# A Director's Guide to the Art of Stand-up

RELATED TITLES

*Disobedient Theatre: Alternative Ways to Inspire, Animate and Play*
By Chris Johnston
ISBN 978-1-350-01454-1

*Getting the Joke*
By Oliver Double
ISBN 978-1-408-17460-9

*Introduction to Arts Management*
By Jim Volz
ISBN 978-1-474-23978-3

*Off the Mic*
By Deborah Frances-White and Marsha Shandur
ISBN 978-1-472-52638-0

*Performing Live Comedy*
By Chris Ritchie
ISBN 978-1-408-14643-9

*Popular Performance*
Edited by Adam Ainsworth, Oliver Double and Louise Peacock
ISBN 978-1-474-24734-4

*The Art of Rehearsal: Conversations with Contemporary Theatre Makers*
Edited by Barbara Simonsen
ISBN 978-1-474-29201-6

# A Director's Guide to the Art of Stand-up

*Chris Head*

*methuen* | drama

LONDON · NEW YORK · OXFORD · NEW DELHI · SYDNEY

METHUEN DRAMA
Bloomsbury Publishing Plc
50 Bedford Square, London, WC1B 3DP, UK

BLOOMSBURY, METHUEN DRAMA and the Methuen Drama logo are trademarks of
Bloomsbury Publishing Plc

First published in Great Britain 2018
Reprinted 2018

Cover design by Adriana Brioso
Cover image © iStock

A catalogue record for this book is available from the British Library.

Library of Congress Cataloging-in-Publication Data
Names: Head, Chris, author.
Title: A director's guide to the art of stand-up comedy / Chris Head.
Description: London; New York: Methuen Drama, [2018] | Includes
bibliographical references and index.
Identifiers: LCCN 2018006481 (print) | LCCN 2018017555 (ebook) | ISBN
9781350035539 (epub) | ISBN 9781350035546 (epdf) | ISBN 9781350035522
(pbk.: alk. paper)
Subjects: LCSH: Stand-up comedy. | Comedy.
Classification: LCC PN1969.C65 (ebook) | LCC PN1969.C65 H43 2018 (print) |
DDC 792.76–dc23
LC record available at https://lccn.loc.gov/2018006481

ISBN: PB: 978-1-350-03552-2
ePDF: 978-1-350-03554-6
eBook: 978-1-350-03553-9

Series: Performance Books

Typeset by Deanta Global Publishing Services, Chennai, India
Printed and bound in Great Britain

To find out more about our authors and books visit www.bloomsbury.com
and sign up for our newsletters.

# CONTENTS

# NOTES ON CONTRIBUTORS

I have conducted twenty-five hours of interviews for this book. I introduce the main interviewees here to save introducing them whenever they join the text.

## Directors, academics and coaches who work with stand-ups

Tony Allen – Author of influential stand-up book *Attitude*, a pioneering stand-up coach and the 'Godfather of Alternative Comedy', Tony was a London Comedy Store regular from its beginnings in 1979 and that year founded *Alternative Cabaret* with Alexei Sayle.

Mr Cee – A stand-up coach who as director worked with Dane Baptiste and the late Felix Dexter. A stand-up in his own right with numerous appearances at the Comedy Store and Hackney Empire, he supported Gina Yashere on her UK tour.

Oliver Double – A comedy academic at the University of Kent and author of the seminal *Getting the Joke*. A former regular on the stand-up circuit, he now performs full-length theatre stand-up shows, most recently *Break A Leg* in 2015.

John Gordillo – One of the leading stand-up directors who has worked with Eddie Izzard, Michael McIntyre and Reginald D. Hunter. In 2015, he directed a live Dylan Moran DVD. As a stand-up, John has performed several critically successful solo shows.

Maggie Inchley – A director and academic, Maggie has directed and developed new plays and is a co-founder of the Comedians Theatre

Company which takes plays to the Edinburgh Fringe with a cast of stand-ups.

**Simon McBurney** – An actor, director and artistic director of theatre company Complicite. He has a strong engagement with comedy, winning the Perrier Comedy Award in Edinburgh in 1985 and directing live shows for French and Saunders and Lenny Henry.

**Dec Munro** – Director of Sofie Hagen's award-winning 2015 Edinburgh show *Bubblewrap* and more recently Andrew Hunter Murray's *Round One* and *The Alasdair Beckett-King Mysteries*. Co-founder of Angel Comedy's Bill Murray venue in London.

**Logan Murray** – A leading stand-up coach and director who has directed *We Are Klang* (featuring Greg Davies) and Milton Jones. He is the author of several books on stand-up including *Be a Great Stand-up*, and performs as Ronnie Rigsby.

**Phil Nichol** – A leading director and also a stand-up, musician and actor, Phil is himself an Edinburgh Fringe regular with the Comedians Theatre Company and his own stand-up story-telling shows including the award-winning *The Naked Racist*.

**Kate Smurthwaite** – A stand-up, director and coach, Kate is a political activist and journalist. She writes for *Have I Got News For You* and *The Revolution Will Be Televised*. With her own stand-up she is an Edinburgh Fringe regular.

**Pat Welsh** – A comedy specialist and senior lecturer at Bath Spa University and a freelance workshop leader and director/performer. He teaches fooling, clowning, improv, commedia and stand-up comedy.

**Phil Whelans** – Directs live comedy including Pippa Evans, Phil Nichol and Stephen Carlin. As a writer, he has a Radio 4 sitcom *My First Planet* and writes and performs with sketch group *Pros from Dover*. He improvises with *Grand Theft Impro*.

# People that I have directed and coached

**Samantha Baines** – A stand-up, writer and actor who has appeared in *The Crown*, *Silent Witness* and *Call the Midwife*, Samantha gigs on the stand-up circuit and performs science-comedy shows – and puns. I worked as director on her 2017 Edinburgh show.

**Eleanor Conway** – A Second City alumni, Eleanor took her first full-length solo stand-up show *Walk of Shame* to the Edinburgh Fringe in 2016, has since toured it nationally and returned with it to the 2017 Fringe at The Stand. I co-directed it.

**Roxy Dunn and Alys Metcalf** – Actors in Channel 4's *Babylon* and *The Play That Goes Wrong* respectively. I directed their comedy play *In Tents and Purposes*, an official sell-out at Edinburgh 2016; it has been toured nationally and performed at Soho Theatre, London.

**Will Gompertz** (author of the foreword) – Will is the BBC's arts editor, a *Guardian* and *Times* journalist and author of *What Are You Looking At?* and *Think Like An Artist*. His 2009 Edinburgh Fringe show was *Double Art History* which I directed.

**Caroline Goyder** – A leading voice coach and author of *Gravitas*. Caroline works with CEOs, TV news anchors and anyone who wants to speak better. A keynote speaker, I directed her in a TEDx talk that at the time of writing has received 4.5 million views.

**Katia Kvinge** – A stand-up, character comic, actor and improviser working in London and LA, Katia has also appeared on BBC3, MTV and Comedy Central. I directed her 2016 Edinburgh show *Squirrel*.

**Richard Lindesay** – A comedy circuit and festival regular with *Fools Suffering Gladly* at the New Zealand International Comedy Festival 2016, and *Nerds, Words and a Clipboard* at the Sydney Fringe Festival 2013. I have coached and directed Richard for several years.

**Hannah Ringham** – Co-founder of performance collective Shunt and a theatre maker and performer, touring internationally, including with Tim Crouch. I worked on her stand-up gigs that were research for her solo theatre show *I Want Love*.

**Steve Whiteley** – An improviser, actor, comedian and YouTuber 'Offkey Steve'. He performs the character Wisebowm, a spoof urban poet/rapper. I direct his Wisebowm shows, which have included those performed at the Edinburgh Fringe in 2016/17.

# Other voices

**Barry Ferns** – A highly regarded emcee, stand-up and co-founder of Angel Comedy in London. Known for his stunts and high-concept shows (like the annual gig at the top of Arthur's Seat). Winner of the Malcolm Hardee and Spirit of the Fringe awards in 2015.

**Zoe Lyons** – A popular circuit and festival stand-up, in 2008 she won the Dave Funniest Joke of The Fringe Award. She has appeared in many TV shows including *Mock the Week*, *The Wright Stuff* and *Michael McIntyre's Comedy Roadshow*.

**Ahir Shah** – A philosophical and political stand-up whose 2016 show *Machines* was seen at the Edinburgh Fringe and Soho Theatre and toured nationally. His 2017 Edinburgh show, *Control*, was nominated for Best Show at the Edinburgh Comedy Awards.

**Mark Thomas** – A stand-up and activist who has performed increasingly theatrical shows including *Bravo Figaro, 100 Acts of Minor Dissent* and *The Red Shed*. His campaigning shows have stopped the building of a dam and changed the law on tax and protest.

**Geoff Whiting** – One of UK's most in-demand compères and a stand-up act with over 5,000 gigs to his name. Through his company Mirth Control he manages stand-up acts and books comics for gigs across the country and internationally.

# PREFACE

This book is the first ever guide to stand-up from the director's perspective. It's based on my work directing and coaching comedians and on many hours of interviews with comedy directors, coaches, academics and with stand-ups themselves. It is for comics, would-be comics and all those who support them and offers tacit, experiential knowledge of stand-up creative processes. In Chapter 11, I discuss the use of the *three-act structure* for full-length stand-up shows. And it is this very structure that I have used for this book. *Act 1* is the opening chapters about the stand-up persona, where ideas come from and how stand-ups and directors work together. *Act 2*, Chapters 4 to 10, is about writing and performing stand-up comedy. *Act 3*, Chapters 11–15, then takes us into the world of full-length festival and touring shows, and finally stand-up moves into theatre.

As well as the three-act structure, I also discuss a stand-up show as potentially having several plot lines. This book has three main plot lines. The *A plot* is the 'guide to stand-up comedy' of the title. Beginning as it does with discovering your voice and identity, newcomers are most welcome. And as it goes right through from open spots, to paid club gigs, to festival shows and beyond, there should be something here for more experienced acts too. The *B plot* is an exploration of the largely undiscussed and growing trend for stand-ups to work with directors. There is a C plot too – how stand-up and theatre relate to and influence each other. This strand is introduced in Chapter 4 with reference to Andrew Scott's 2017 Hamlet and then itself takes centre stage in Chapters 14 and 15. And as is the way of classic plotting, all three plotlines collide in the final chapter.

Interweaved with my thoughts you will find insights from directors and coaches who have worked with acts at every level of

stand-up from open spots, to club comics, to festival and touring
acts, to TV comics and internationally famous stand-ups. Above
all, for stand-ups, this book is an opportunity to get a director's
perspective on your work for a fraction of the price of working with
one in the flesh.

# FOREWORD

Chris Head is hilarious. He takes comedy so seriously. For him, it is an academic subject. He is a professor of the pun, a connoisseur of the callback; an A-star student of stand-up. When he's watching a top comedian banging out punchlines quicker than Trump tweets, he doesn't laugh, he doesn't even smile ... he takes notes. Or strokes his chin.

Chris can – and with the smallest encouragement, will – explain in forensic detail the formal structural components of a Bill Hicks routine. He will analyse with the precision of a German engineer the shape-shifting beats of an anthropomorphic act-out, or the basic rules of a classic set-up and payoff gag. His comedy knowledge is encyclopaedic, his earnest enthusiasm for the subject, contagious. I know this. I have first-hand experience.

It was back in the noughties when I was writing an article for the *Guardian* newspaper about the many crimes committed against the English language by museum curators when producing texts about art for public consumption; I thought it would be interesting to explore a different approach to the problematic task of trying to explain the complexities of art without reverting to incomprehensible technical jargon, or pomposity, or both. So I enrolled on a stand-up comedy course, reasoning that one of the many skills a comedian must have is an ability to communicate essential, often complex, information in an entertaining, accessible way.

This was before the comedy boom, a time before the professionalization of stand-up; it was in the dark ages of spit-and-sawdust pubs and rancid subterranean clubs when evening courses for wannabe comedians were as rare as a contrite banker. Eventually though, after a lot of asking around, I was pointed in the direction of a pub on Leather Lane, London. It was a Tuesday evening in early summer and the place was empty save for a grumpy-looking barman who told me, 'If you're after a bloke who looks like Jesus Christ, he's upstairs.' I ascended.

The room was as bereft of punters as the bar below. The aesthetic was ascetic. There were no pictures, no carpets and no furniture. Except, that is, for eight wooden stools, a single mic on a stand (unplugged), and a rickety old chair, upon which sat a man who looked like Jesus Christ. He seemed to be in his own private zone. I was about to leave. But then Christ spoke to me.

'Hello, I'm Chris', he said, modestly dropping the 't'.

'I might grab a beer', I replied.

'Maybe after the class.' He said, 'The others will be here in a minute.'

I sat on a stool.

It didn't strike me at the time as a life-changing moment, but it was. Over the course of the next ten Tuesday evenings I learnt how to construct, frame and present spoken-word content in a way that felt not only authored but also authentic. By which I mean, specifically written for me by me. I know, it sounds simple, but it isn't.

Self-awareness is all well and good, but in comedy specifically – and in verbal communication more generally – it is essential that the performer/speaker understands how he or she is perceived by the audience. This is not something you can judge for yourself (you can try, but you'll be wrong); you need the eyes and ears of others, as I found out on Chris's course. What I discovered came as a big surprise.

I won't go into the details of how he helped me and the rest of the class find our individual 'voices'; it is all laid out in splendid prose by the man himself in the opening chapters. But I will say that it is but one of the enlightening insights he gave us into the art of performance. For me, it opened up a world that I didn't know before and haven't stopped exploring since. I hope this book does something similar for you.

*Will Gompertz, BBC Arts Editor*
*(A Joker Sage in Chris's Archetypes – see Chapter 1)*

*Author's note:*
*I have since had a haircut and no longer resemble the Messiah.*

# ACKNOWLEDGEMENTS

Enormous thanks are due to all the directors and stand-ups who have kindly taken the time to speak to me for the book. Thanks to their input, it is a hugely richer volume than it would have been otherwise.

Thank you to my stupendous wife Kate Dineen for all her suggestions and ideas. This book would not exist without her support, encouragement and tolerance of me disappearing for hours on end to work on it. (And for the record, she is the true begetter of the 'stand-up levels' model at the end of Chapter 2.)

Thank you to Raphy Mendoza for designing the two images in the text. Thanks too to Dave's Funniest Joke of the Fringe award for giving me permission to quote winning and shortlisted one-liners in Chapters 5, 6 and 10. And particular thanks are due to my commissioning editor and reviewers at Methuen Drama who, when I proposed a 'how to' book, suggested instead that I write from the director's perspective. (It seems so obvious now.)

Finally, this book is born out of thousands of hours of directing, workshops and consultations. My thanks go to all the comedians I have worked with over the years.

# ACT 1

# On-stage identity/off-stage process

# 1

# Directing the persona:

# The comedic self

Stand-up comedy. It's the ultimate solo art form, isn't it?

Actually, no. If you're already doing stand-up, you'll be used to having plenty of outside input. If you're considering doing stand-up (and who isn't, these days?) you'll find that you can't develop your work in isolation. Who are to be your 'outside eyes'? First: audiences. They give you unambiguous feedback of a direct and simple kind. Then there are other comics, who are often generous with their ideas and insights. Perhaps you have an agent; they can be a varied bunch, who range from being controlling to laissez-faire. A coach perhaps to get you started, and periodically sharpen your act. Maybe a co-writer. And increasingly there's the stand-up comedy director.

## The director in the shadows

'What do you do?' people ask me. 'I direct stand-up comedians,' I say. This is only one facet of my work, but it's certainly one that gets a reaction. And the reaction it often gets is: 'How on earth can you direct stand-up?' It's as if I've said 'I direct conversations that people have down the pub.' This reaction is perhaps unsurprising. For while directing in theatre and film calls attention to itself and is admired and analysed, stand-up directing is so self-effacing that the audience usually has no idea that a director is involved; indeed, stand-up directors are sometimes not even credited on flyers, posters or DVD covers. And even when an audience is aware of the shadowy presence of a director, they'd be hard-pressed to say what it was they did. In short, a stand-up director can be a combination of all of the above 'outside eyes'. They are a sympathetic and critical audience, often (but not always) a fellow comic; like an agent they can have your career and personal well-being in mind, and, particularly when they're working with new acts, they can be a coach too. They'll hone and guide your performance, and they can even write for you. It can be a highly collaborative process. The role of stand-up director was relatively obscure until recently, with the likes of Chris Rock directing Amy Schumer, and in the UK, Noel Fielding directing Paul Foot.[1] And yet, more and more comics are working with directors at all levels from open spots and club gigs, to festival shows, tours and DVDs.

Stand-up directing has in part grown out of the relatively recent phenomenon of stand-up courses. I've run a stand-up course above a pub in central London for ten years, initially on Leather Lane and then shifting west to Soho. Several acts I've directed in festival shows first worked with me on that course. (Including BBC arts editor Will Gompertz, who kindly wrote the foreword for this book.) In many ways, the stand-up coach is an act's first director.

So, let's begin in the classroom by considering how the director can help the newer comic find their identity and help the more experienced comic develop and exploit theirs. And we'll soon progress out into comedy clubs and eventually, in the final section of the book, we'll be working on full-length festival and touring shows.

## The comedic persona

Why work on your stand-up persona? First, audiences don't laugh *at material*, they laugh with, or sometimes at, the person who is performing. The identity, style and personality of the individual on stage is fundamental in stand-up. Your stand-up persona could be a more upbeat, lively you. It may be a more downbeat, cynical you. Often there is funniness in negative traits and failings.

Think about how Amy Schumer finds comedy in her sexual misadventures. Stand-ups typically find their persona by going on stage, performing and seeing what the audience respond to. A well-known example is Jack Dee only finding his persona when he was disillusioned and on the verge of giving up. He did his first open spot in 1988. Going on stage at the Comedy Store with no material he nevertheless got some laughs from ad-libbing and playing around with the audience. Encouraged, he gigged on the circuit with a chatty, upbeat persona while working in unfulfilling jobs, but found little success. Disillusioned and ready to quit, he took to the stage with a grumpy, couldn't-care-less attitude, and it worked. More recently, Bridget Christie spent many years exclusively performing as various characters and only truly found her voice when she started performing as herself. Amy Schumer is another act who has been getting closer to her real self on stage, but she still sees a distinction between her on-stage self and off-stage self. She acknowledges that having started with an on-stage character who was an 'irreverent, kind of privileged idiot', now 'the two ladies' are getting closer and closer together as she becomes more herself on stage.[2] So even though Schumer's persona is becoming closer to who she really is, they will never become one-and-the-same person.

For other comedians, however, rather than finding their voice as they become closer to their real selves, they travel in the opposite direction. One-liner comic Milton Jones says he used to go on as himself and sometimes it would work and sometimes it wouldn't. But then he found that if he messed his hair up and put on a silly jumper, or latterly a loud shirt, then it acted as a signpost, and people suddenly got it. He says that as soon as he thought of his on-stage self as a character, he became easier to write for.[3]

Sometimes performers adopt an entirely fictional stand-up comedy character which they might perform exclusively, or alongside an act they perform as 'themselves'. How might a stand-up character develop? Sometimes the character allows the comic to say things that would not be possible if they appeared as themselves. Or a character can simply be an attacking parody of things the comic doesn't like. It can also, however, be the case that there is some affection in the character, with it drawing on something real about the stand-up's life and their enthusiasms. For example, Al Murray read Modern History at Oxford, and his knowledge of history is cheerfully warped by the Pub Landlord's Little Englander outlook. Alexis Dubus, who performs as absurdly self-regarding Frenchman Marcel Lucont, is a Francophile and fluent French speaker. I am currently directing Steve Whiteley as the urban poet/ rap character Wisebowm. As with all comic characters, there is a heavy dose of dramatic irony. The comedy, however, doesn't come from inept music or rhyming; both are very skilfully executed. The comedy comes from his delusions of profundity; he sees himself as a profound lyricist and thinker – the audience considers him banal and absurd. The beginnings of the character have roots in Steve's youthful enthusiasms. 'As a seventeen-year-old, I was really into the Garage scene. I'd got turntables and a microphone, and I'd emcee – much to the annoyance of my parents.' The fact that he loved that world makes for a more rounded or more affectionate character than if he was just mocking people. Even when you are performing as 'yourself', it can be beneficial to think of your *on-stage self* as a character: It is your comedic self. That way there is some distance between the actual you and the stand-up you. In effect, you have someone you are portraying and writing *for* who is distinct from your everyday self. Defining this on-stage character helps find the angle you'll take on any given topic and the kind of jokes and material you'll write for yourself. Whether an act is presenting a stand-up self that is close to their real self or adopting a more fictionalized character, there needs to be a measure of authenticity. Those early audiences didn't buy the upbeat Jack Dee, but they did believe the disgruntled Dee. Pat Welsh describes this on-stage persona as 'one authentic self': 'I'm interested in work that's been done with chief executives about these authentic selves. For example, I read a paper about an Afro-Caribbean music mogul sitting on a record label board of directors. When he works with his primarily white, middle-class colleagues, he presents one persona, but when he's working with young black musicians he shows a different self. And *both* are authentic.' In comedy, Pat calls it 'the comedic self'.

## Directing an act's persona

An exploration of the stand-up's persona has to begin with the real person. Tony Allen remarked to me, 'Some people don't like it when comedians become actors, but I think the problem is when actors become comedians. They *do* a comedian. They don't find the comedian in themselves; they do an actor doing a comedian.' As a director or a coach, how does one set about helping an act find the comedian in themselves? The primary means is *reflecting back* to the performer what it is they are doing. I see this as one of my primary roles as director. Oliver Double described to me the early stages of working with new student stand-ups:

> A lot of the things I do with them are essentially diagnostic. One of the first things I'll do is get them in front of a microphone talking to the rest of the group as an audience. That's like a magnifying glass for the personality. You notice things about them that you wouldn't in a more everyday interaction. Maybe there's a tiny little speech impediment; maybe there are gestures that are very *them*. Maybe there's a bit of a posh accent, or there's a slight camp pitch to their voice, or there's a northern twang that you hadn't spotted. I mean they're small things really, but if 'self is text' you need to understand what the tone of that text is, and that's facial expression, gestures, vocabulary, quirks. I always report those back to a student, and I'd point out where they are helpful and where they're not.

Something Oliver identifies is laughing at your own material: 'It *can* be really helpful. There are lots of comedians that do that. But in other cases, it can be a sign of insecurity and, if it's done with some awkwardness, it can detract.' A comic I have worked with can produce a very convincing little chuckle. He has found that if he uses it when he sets up a comic premise, it can help the audience start laughing too. And a laugh can help a payoff. For instance, Dave Chappelle, after he's delivered an outrageous punchline, will step back, let his hand with the mic drop so that it hits his leg, and laugh. This allows him some distance from the idea and enables him and the audience to laugh together, often in disbelief, at what has come out of his mouth. Laughs, however, can detract if the comedy of the act is dependent on them being deadpan – although the audience can enjoy it when the mask slips a little.

When I reflect back their persona as I see it to stand-ups, I look at it from a number of perspectives. I wouldn't necessarily consider all of them, every time, but I have found these are useful areas to feed back on:

Archetype
Attitude
Likeability
Shadow
Struggle
Status
Self-awareness
The act's look

Let's work through these in turn, beginning with archetypes. If you work with acts, you might like to work through this checklist with a stand-up. If you are an act, you can get someone else to reflect back their observations of you under these categories, or you can watch a video of yourself and consider them.

# Archetypes

First, I find a useful way into the persona can be to think of an act in terms of the twelve Jungian archetypes. There are several versions of these online, but I've found these have a good fit with stand-up:

*the innocent, the regular person, the crusader, the caregiver, the explorer, the rebel, the sensualist, the creator, the jester, the sage, the magician* and *the ruler.*[4]

From a stand-up perspective: *the innocent* is the naive optimist (Lee Evans and Brian Regan). *The regular person* is a mate of the audience (Michael McIntyre or Sarah Millican). *The crusader* is political and campaigning (Mark Thomas and Josie Long). *The caregiver* has real concern for their audience and the wider world (Josie Long again and in his surreal way Paul Foot who expresses concern for the audience's comfort and organizes a fan club with perks for 'the connoisseurs'). *The explorer* actively investigates the world and reports back (Dave Gorman and Samantha Baines). *The rebel* breaks the rules and challenges social norms (Sarah Silverman and Denis Leary). *The sensualist* focuses on sex and pleasures (Amy Schumer and Russell Brand). *The creator* brings other aspects to the stand-up performance from music to art (Demetri Martin and Simon Munnery). *The jester* is the one-liner comic (Steven Wright and Milton Jones). *The sage* is the thoughtful, philosophical stand-up (Bill Hicks and Russell Brand again). *The magician* makes the impossible possible in their concepts and imagery (Eddie Izzard and Noel Fielding). *The ruler* is the alpha comic, the funniest and sharpest (Chris Rock and Amy Schumer again).

These archetypes become particularly useful for stand-up when used in combination. For example, Russell Brand already crops up twice in my examples, making him a *sensualist sage*, and also appearing twice is Amy Schumer, a *sensualist ruler*. The combined archetypes add depth and breadth and also set up a potentially comic friction between the two qualities. For example, Bill Hicks could be considered a *rebel sage*. (In a recent stand-up class of mine, the group reflected back to one participant that he was a *sensualist joker*. Concerned, he asked, 'Are you saying I'm a joke in bed?') Finding the archetypes that fit an act can be an opening to understanding the persona.

## Attitudes

I asked Tony Allen how he applies his own work on attitude in practice and he explained: 'I concentrate on *who* people are when they're on stage. Oliver Double always says my best line [from his book *Attitude*] is "When you're in front of an audience a strategic identity crisis takes place." And that's who you're left with on stage because all the other parts of your personality, they just clear off, they're not having any of it. They could be really low-status parts. You could be standing there,' he pulls a pathetic, fearful face, 'and that's perfect because that'll keep you there.' He told me that in class after someone has performed in front of the group he says, 'Who was that up there? What did you see? Give me some adjectives to describe them. Even if you saw it for a few seconds, put it down.' And to the performer, 'Write them all down. That's your palette, your cluster of attitudes.'

Tony said he also always asks a new comic where they're from and then reflects back the attitude of their response. He did it with me! He asked, 'Where are you from?' and I responded in a pleased, upbeat way, 'Well I was born in Brighton!' And he replied, 'The way you said that was "*Brighton!*", chirpy and proud. So, I'd give you back that information; that it was perky and bright. You wouldn't have picked up that thing I gave you there.' And he was right; I wouldn't have. He went on, 'Okay, so normally it's the other way round. People's attitude is more: "*bloody place*." But you did it chipper so I'd go with that.' He then illustrated how this might play out in a performance. '"My name's Chris Head"' he said downbeat, then switching the tone, '"and I was born in Brighton!" And immediately they're laughing – there's two. There's "*My name's Chris Head*" and it's perfunctory and there's "*Brighton!!*"'

It's significant here that Tony found two attitudes and switched between them. For comedy, you need two things in comic friction. Here, these two attitudes would be drawn from the 'palette'. The key to this is that there needs to be a mix of attitudes, both positive and negative. You are seeking contrasts: 'You choose what to use and what opposites to construct jokes with. Your attitude is that combination. I directed [stand-up poet] Johnny Fluffy Punk's show *Man Up*. Johnny has this exasperated sort of born-to-lose underachieving low status but with a passion and an anger about it.' So, a contrast between low-energy resignation and high-energy defiance. 'My thing is that in drama the conflict is between characters and in stand-up, the clash is within the self. It's the internal conflict you're revealing to the audience. And that's why it's an art form. Standing up and doing jokes all night is not an art form. It's just doing a script aloud'.

As the funniness is the mix of attitudes, I asked Tony what he'd do if a new comic was only displaying positive attitudes. He said: 'I'll ask questions. I'll say, "So have you had sex with your mother?" And they go: "No!!!" And I'll say, "Okay what we got there is absolute effrontery."' Here he has forced an attitude that could be a fruitful contrast. He adds, 'We want to see what they're like under pressure, because they're going to be under pressure in front of an audience. Someone is going to call them a "cunt." And how do they deal with that? Do they get feminist about it? Or dogmatic and earnest?' And pressure situations in life will be sources of material and their attitude in these situations will be a fundamental aspect of their persona. He goes on, 'When you go on [stage], it helps if you give them a hint of all the edges you've got. If you go on and the first thing you say is, "For fuck's sake ... no sorry, I won't start like that." You've already seen he can go right *up there* and he can go right *down there*. If in your opening few seconds you're hinting at your extremes, you're establishing who you are.'

# Likeability

When I direct a stand-up, I ask myself: Why are they likeable? This question could be easy to answer. It may be more of a challenge. If you can't find anything, you probably shouldn't be directing them. When it comes to likeability, acts exist on a spectrum from straightforwardly likeable to nasty, with ironically the nasty acts finding an audience that do like them (for example Frankie Boyle) and the likeable acts often finding a vocal minority who dislike them. (Michael McIntyre being a case in point.) Where a comic is overwhelmingly negative, perhaps there is something about their rebelliousness, recklessness, charm or sheer front that is appealing and enables at least some people to warm to them.

When we spoke, John Gordillo argued: 'The bottom line is, we're not going to laugh at your jokes, and we're not going to care about your story unless we like and connect with you. It's not about being likeable for the sake of it. It's about being likeable to get to the funny part of the idea and to make your point. It's in the same way that socially you need to like someone before you want to listen to them.'

How can a director or coach help an act find their likeability? First, you can identify and encourage self-deprecation in their act. The simple art of mocking yourself can be a shortcut to the audience liking you. It has multiple benefits, and if you can laugh at yourself, then the audience knows that they can laugh at you too. (And often the very negative or sick comics are equally hard on themselves.) When you have mocked yourself, you are then more at liberty to mock others. You also might have headed off potential hecklers by getting in first. Showing vulnerability is also an effective way to build likeability into the act, particularly if the comic is otherwise very strident.

While your negative emotions are the funny ones, your positive emotions can help create a likeable and relatable persona. In his directing, Mr Cee told me that he works on developing authentic

emotions and having a more heart-based connection with the
audience and the material:

> One of most challenging things I've found with directing
> comedians is getting them to tap into real emotion. Yes, they've
> got gags but you can't tell *who* they are as a person. I think
> the modern audience wants to feel that they know that person
> on stage, that they can relate to them. For me now, when I'm
> teaching and directing, it's about: 'How can you connect
> emotionally with what you're saying? I know it's a *joke* about
> your relationship, but what do you want people to think about
> you and your partner? There *is* love there, so display the love,
> have that balance. Your audience then understands you a lot
> better.' I think from that you create a better following.

# Shadow

Thinking about acts' negative sides and developing the idea of
the persona, we might add a 'shadow'. This helps me find the two
levels that will contrast with each other and create a comic friction.
Again, adapted from Jungian ideas, in this simple model of persona/
shadow, the shadow is all the stuff that contradicts and undermines
the persona. We then have two levels, one contrasting with the
other and with an opportunity to switch between them. If someone
is overwhelmingly shadow I am looking for that cheek or charm
that will offset it.

Take Sarah Silverman. Her sweet-natured persona is sharply
contradicted by the shadow side that pours forth. The same goes
for Sarah Millican. Sarah Silverman's persona might be described
as innocent and her shadow is her shocking, dark streak. The
contrast between the content and the attitude creates a funny
friction and what's more the innocence enables us to like her
despite the content.

When I work with comics, I always say that in stand-up your
imperfections, like Jack Dee's grumpiness, can be your strength.
Most comics have shared, played with and even celebrated their
negative sides. A director can help you identify the 'failings'
that work for your persona then you can exaggerate them and
consciously write for this heightened version of yourself.

On my stand-up course, I ask my students to think of a person who knows them well and has an emotional attachment to them, such as a partner, sibling or parent. I then ask them to think about how their failings annoy that person, which always generates much hilarity. You are looking at this awful version of yourself from an outside perspective, and it's funny. Try it for yourself. What three adjectives would someone close to you use to describe *you* when you're annoying? A recent example was a new comic whose partner would describe him as 'childish, stubborn and untidy'. There was a lot of laughter as the group considered these adjectives. The participants then took it in turns to go up to the microphone and, in the manner of an upbeat emcee, introduce *themselves* using these adjectives as if they were positive qualities. In this case: 'Ladies and gentlemen, the next act is childish, stubborn and untidy! Please welcome to the stage...' (If you're wondering about my own three, they're: 'pompous, disorganized and passive aggressive'.) The fun and illuminating thing about this simple exercise is that the three negative adjectives tend to elicit the response: 'Oh this is going to be good.' We relish people sharing their dysfunctions in stand-up. Interestingly, childishness, stubbornness and untidiness hadn't featured at all in this particular performer's act. (Maybe in his behaviour before and after the gig, but not on stage.) This gave him pause. He realized that he had been missing a massive opportunity and this set him on a fruitful path of rethinking his existing material and looking into where else he could go with it.

# Struggle

I once worked with a man who had a terror of public speaking. He had been publicly humiliated when he'd gotten confused and into a muddle in a presentation at university. All of this angst fell away when he discovered that he could deliberately and artfully become confused and muddled in his stand-up act. He even ended up making a routine out of the original humiliation which was wonderfully cathartic. His struggle with speaking became the content.

Sarah Millican struggles with her appetite – she can't pass a cake shop. We know we are allowed to laugh, so it's funny. If a comic on stage struggled with their weight but was trying to hide it or was denying it and we knew it would be off limits for our laughter, at the very least they'd be missing a trick. Looked at in the right light – with permission to laugh established – your struggles can be a great topic for stand-up.

I worked via Skype with a new comedian based in Denmark. She shared with me a video of an early five-minute set. In it, she started off as a pure oddball, then angry, then became upbeat, and then a downbeat, introspective, depressive sort of character. All in five minutes! She hadn't thought about how her character was changing; she was just trying to be funny. By starting off in this oddball persona – almost a North European, female Emo Philips (which I admit sounds promising) – she set up expectations that weren't then met by how the set went on. The changes in her character that followed were just confusing. As an audience member, you had to keep re-finding your feet with an act that you thought you had understood. We talked over her persona and found that the oddball wasn't her and that she'd have trouble sustaining it. The anger was okay but not authentic – she didn't really feel angry about those topics. Anger can be brilliant when you feel it, but often if it's fake it won't ring true and then won't be funny. An exception to this is when the anger is comically misplaced as in when you rage over something trivial that doesn't merit such fury. Even here though there needs to be a kernel of truth; we recognize the stand-up probably does have a short fuse in real life, albeit not to this absurd degree.

The depressive character, on the other hand, was authentic to her and had worked in the performance. More importantly, she could see opportunities and angles for writing further material with this characteristic to the fore. And yet she didn't feel she could be consistently lifeless and downbeat. It may well be possible to do a thoroughly miserable character and still have the audience enjoy it: perhaps more as a character portrayal or perhaps enjoying the absurdity of the emotion taken to that degree, but it certainly would be monotonous and limited. Seeking two levels to her persona, we hit upon the solution of her trying to be upbeat but constantly being undermined by her depressive side. This struggle, this inner conflict, has more potential for comedy. In presenting a positive aspect that is undermined by the negative it gives her the opportunity to switch between the two.

Even struggling with *stand-up* can be used to comic effect. For example, you might have problems with your high-pitched delivery. Where a public speaking tutor would want to address this, in stand-up it could be a vital part of your funniness, as is the case for

Bobcat Goldthwaite. Even being bad at stand-up itself can be part of the act. The challenge here is letting the audience in on the joke since they may think you are genuinely incompetent! For example, I helped an older comic develop a character act of an old-school mainstream comic who was losing his marbles (shades of Count Arthur Strong), but the trouble was he was so convincing some audiences didn't realize it was an act! We choreographed this lovely piece of physical comedy which led to one promoter complaining: 'Never book this man for my gig again. He was so hopeless he even got tangled up in the mic lead.' The classic example of this 'anti-comedy' is notorious US maverick, Andy Kaufman. More recently Ed Aczel and Gregg Turkington as his character Neil Hamburger have carved out similar territory for themselves.

Moreover, profound physical and mental challenges with performance can be turned to the performer's advantage. I once had a student who had a brain injury, which had led him to struggle with his speech. Initially, we were caught up in thinking 'Oh God, poor guy.' But once he'd learnt to gives us permission to laugh about it, we could relax, and he could then use this idiosyncrasy as an aspect of his funniness in his act. Francesca Martinez does the same thing with her cerebral palsy. She'd spent years feeling that to be accepted she had to hide her differences, but on stage, she found that being 'open and relaxed about who she was' led to acceptance. She says, 'It felt incredibly empowering.'[5] One of the truly great and liberating things about stand-up is the way it alchemizes the negatives into positives.

# Status

An act will also have a status that they project. I work with three status levels: high status, low status and in between – the audience's mate. Acts don't always have a sense of their status, so I help them identify and play up to it. What status are you?

A high-status act looks down on the problems of the world and life from a lofty position of insight and wit. But they are not perfect. In one way or another, high-status comics often come with a significant dose of self-deprecation and awareness of their own failings. A great example is Richard Pryor, and another is Amy Schumer. Being high status can present problems for a British comic. In Britain, there is a culture of wanting to knock winners down rather than celebrating them. So, if a British comic is setting themselves up as sharp, intelligent or successful they often quite intentionally lower their status. Stewart Lee is a case in point: 'In order to say lots of what I say, and not appear like an arrogant bully, I have to be low status on some level.'[6]

In audience's mate status, you are like their funny, outspoken friend. Michael McIntyre and Sarah Millican are examples of audience mates. The act creates laughs of recognition, and they share your pain. This is probably the most common status. Low-status act are put upon by the problems of the world and life and are struggling with them. If the high-status comic is better than the audience, then the low-status one is worse. Examples of low-status comics are Lee Evans (the struggling type) and Irish comic Kevin McAleer (cheerfully unaware of how odd he is).

These three status levels are then, once again, enriched when used in combination. We might consider an act in terms of two status levels, one primary and one secondary. Doug Stanhope is high status (primary) due to his intelligence and control over his performance, but the picture of his life he presents is often extremely low status (secondary). It's not just high-status comics bringing in a secondary low-status strand, however. Sarah Millican has an audience's mate likeability (primary) but the portrait of herself she too presents is often low status (secondary). Meanwhile, Lee Evans is low status (primary) but is beloved by his audience and so is also the audience's mate (secondary).

# Self-awareness

As an aid to writing and developing material, Kate Smurthwaite brings the analysis of the act's style back to the comic:

> I would look at what somebody has got and say, 'Okay, it seems like you have a style. Let's play into that, let's make the most of that'. And a director may also be able to see your work in a way that you don't see it. For example, with one comic I said: 'I would describe your work as faux-naive.' It might be that they don't necessarily see what it is they're doing. They just know, 'I act like this and I get a laugh', and once you can analyse it, they can do it more, they can do it deliberately, and they can do it on new subjects in a new way.

*And* they can then reverse it. Once they have a clearly established persona, at times, they can play against it.

Faux-naivety is playing with a lack of self-awareness. The high-status likes of Doug Stanhope are very self-aware. Low-status acts can differ in their awareness levels – Lee Evans is aware of his failings, and that adds pathos to his struggles. In a very different comic world, low-status Milton Jones is oblivious to how mad he is. How self-aware is *your* on-stage persona? In 2008, I saw Kevin McAleer perform a wonderful one-hour set as part of a Stewart Lee-curated run of shows at the Bloomsbury Theatre in London. McAleer's entire show was based on the audience seeing that he was a weird oddball causing people problems, but McAleer himself thought everyone else was to blame. This is dramatic irony as Stewart Lee discusses:

> As far as dramatic irony goes, you're seeing one thing, but another thing is happening – that's what I think interesting stand-up is all about and Kevin McAleer, whom I love, is a master of this. Essentially, he tells very monotonous stories in such a way that it seems he doesn't understand their implications. He speaks as if he is actually angered by the reactions of everyone around him, who are, in fact, behaving quite reasonably. He doesn't seem to understand what they're doing, and yet it's obvious to us, the audience, that they're trying to help. He becomes increasingly frustrated with them, and talks to us as if all these reasonable people are idiots. Kevin McAleer, the man, knows what he's doing, but the character on stage is a different thing.[7]

Here we open up a niche aspect of self-awareness: Is your on-stage character even aware that they are doing a comedy performance, or is your character just talking about the world and their life without meaning to be funny? I once had a student who was taking this kind of low-status oddball stance. It became evident to me that the moments where he referred to his 'jokes' detracted from the feeling that this weird person had just wandered up and started talking about his life. It's not that the audience didn't know it was an act, it just worked better if the act didn't seem to know it was an act!

Jack Dee is another example of a high-status act, but who undercuts his status, partly through dramatic irony: 'You're blaming everyone else for your problems and can't see that, in fact, you are to blame. I've always found that very amusing, and it's always been a big part of my stage persona. There's nothing funnier than someone who thinks life has colluded against him, someone who believes that everyone has got it in for him. That's not a rare comic attribute, Woody Allen is the master of that style of comedy, and it works brilliantly for me.'[8]

# The act's look

What an act wears is an essential part of their persona. An 'audience mate' act like Russell Howard tends to dress like his audience. Geoff Whiting observed, 'He always wears a T-shirt and jeans, and that's become his look.' And high-status Jimmy Carr had his look from the start. Geoff recalled, 'He did his second ever gig for me, his second five minutes. And he was in exactly what he wears now: an immaculate suit with a floral shirt. He had it at the start, and he's never changed.' But sometimes a change in look can make a big difference. As we have seen, Milton Jones arrived at a look that was pivotal in making his act work. Geoff recalled:

> About a year, a year-and-a-half in, Milton found this look with his hair spiked up with hair gel and with a pullover, either with a reindeer on the front or brightly coloured. Usually inappropriate. In the summer, he'd be wearing a Christmas pullover. Since he's become better known, he's switched to multi-coloured shirts, but he's basically stuck with the same look for about twenty-two years. It worked for him because sometimes people would say to me, 'Can you book that chap who does the one-liners?' I'd say, 'Who do you mean?' and they'd say, 'The bloke that wears the funny pullovers.' That's why I tell acts to find a look. New comics don't realize how important that can be.

# 2

# Where comic ideas come from (and how to cultivate them)

Now we've explored the identity of the stand-up, let's consider the slippery question of coming up with funny ideas. I asked Logan Murray, 'Where *do* comic ideas come from?' and he responded, 'I asked that question in Shanghai and someone said "from the internet," but it doesn't answer the question, it just pushes it down a level.' The creative process tends to consist of turning an idea over in your mind, asking questions, forgetting about it and then ... when you're doing something else ... suddenly: *an idea*. This leap is a result of preparing the ground for inspiration to emerge from the subconscious. Given that the subconscious is by its nature inaccessible to the conscious mind, exactly what's going on down there remains mysterious. Nevertheless, we can see that a creative process has time feeding the subconscious and then time allowing it to do its (mysterious) work.

When we spoke, Logan had given his students some stimulus for their creative minds: 'I just printed out sheets [of questions] today for the group I'm working with. I wish somebody told me this. Rather than staring at a blank piece of paper and trying to force something, give yourself some idiot problems that demand stupid answers like: "Things not to say to a girlfriend's parents." Another one says: "How do you tell a child their pet has died? Stick them up on bits of paper all around the house, then when you walk past you can think about it, then you go off and do something else." This plants the question in the subconscious. *What must not be said to a girlfriend's parents? How would I tell a child their pet has died?'*

In their third year at Bath Spa University, Pat Welsh takes acting students through the process of performing a stand-up piece. The aim is to find their 'comedic selves'. Pat discussed the 'elephant in the room', the thing about the performer that will immediately strike an audience: 'It could be someone who has got a limp or a broad Scottish accent. It can be difficult to negotiate. And also, it's context defined. Where I teach, the area is mostly white and middle class and so on the whole is the student body. So, when you have someone of ethnicity that stands out. Now I don't want always to be pushing "play the ethnic card," but if that's the elephant in the room you've either got to address that or come in with something so strong that that's forgotten.'

Pat gets the student on stage and goes into a process of questioning them, 'I start with: tell me ten things I don't know about you. I then pick one and – using that exercise from Tony Allen's *Attitude* I say "Let's double-click on that." [Let's question and explore that further.] And then I interrogate them, and I act as a provocateur, in the spirit of John Wright and Gaulier. I get them to talk about that, and then the question is: How can we get you to accentuate that aspect of yourself?'

Pat told me about a current student of his, a young black woman, who had been frustrated that she kept ending up as 'the sassy black Beyoncé type'. 'Then [through the questioning process] she found an obsessive strand – she likes things very organized.' Pat asked her if this comes out in her eating, perhaps expecting some rigid dietary requirements but instead discovered that 'even when she eats, the food has to be organized on the plate. The chips here, the peas over there. And I said if you come in with that you don't need to play the black card. We forget about everything else, and that's the thing we go for.' Here an unexpected aspect of the student's persona has been discovered, which in this case could well include 'sassy Beyoncé type' *and* 'anal obsessive'. It is with this kind of combination that comic sparks can fly. When Kate Smurthwaite works with new stand-ups on developing material she will invite them to look at a thought from several angles:

I get them to comment in different voices. For instance, I'll say, 'Okay, you've written *I went on holiday to Spain.* What does a stupid child think about that? "Spain is a sunny place that is on the TV." How about an angry middle-aged person going through a divorce?' And they'll say, 'Well, I went to bloody Spain because there are no decent men left in Britain.' I'll say, 'Okay great. What does a massive geek think about this? "I want to fly as far south as possible in a straight line to maximize the efficiency of the journey without actually holidaying in the sea."' Then I'll say, 'What does an alien think? "Why do humans travel halfway across the world to relax? What an odd way to behave."' Even, if necessary I'll say 'What does somebody who's taken LSD think? "Spain is where all the unicorns are."' By just going through that process, sometimes with ten or twenty different voices, my theory is one of those voices might be your punchline.

Through this process, Kate is inviting the stand-up to answer questions playfully. Play is the starting point of funny ideas. Judgement inhibits play, so don't censor or be critical about what you are producing. Simply enjoy posing questions and answering them in surprising ways. Comedy, and all creativity, begins with questions. What takes you into comedic territory, rather than literary or dramatic territory, is that your answers are absurd or playful or perverse. Here are questions that you can usefully ask of any topic you have chosen to talk about:

*What's it like? Any playful analogy you can think of?*

*What next? How bad is it going to get?*

*What before? How did this come about?*

*What isn't it like? (Maybe it's not as you're told it should be.)*

*What should it be like?*

*What would you love them to do?*

*What's it like for them/it? (Put yourselves in their shoes – the 'it' is an invitation to personification – see Chapter 7.)*

*What are they thinking?*

*What if it were reversed? (e.g. the kids are teaching.)*

*What if it were planned? (Rather than it being random, imagine it was organized and set up.)*

> *What if it were in another context? (Same behaviour, different place; e.g. if it's in public, what if they were at home?)*
>
> *What would you love to do? (To get revenge or turn the tables or make a point?)*
>
> *What would solve it?*

Questions like these are often at the genesis of comic ideas. The stand-up brain is always questioning, and these questions are instructions to the subconscious to start its work. Let's say your topic is: supermarket self-service checkouts. This is perhaps overdone as a subject, but it's not necessarily about finding a new topic, it's more about finding your own angle.

> What next? *They'll have self-grow food and just sell seeds.*
>
> What before? *They must have seen an especially patient member of the public showing a new member of staff how to do his job and thought 'the customers are better at working check-outs than our staff. Why don't we get them to do it?'*

Notice this question-and-answer approach naturally drops into a set-up/payoff rhythm – the question being the set-up and the answer being the payoff. Stand-up can really fly when things are hypothetical or speculative. You don't have to stick with talking about how things are, but can focus instead on 'How could they be?' or 'How did they come to be?' As well as these kinds of general questions, you will also want to ask specific questions. Here you might ask: *Who recorded the voice? What if it were someone else? Who would I love it to be? Who designed the system?*

In the classic Bill Hicks 'Positive Drugs story' from his final special *Revelations*,[1] he criticizes the news for only ever reporting negative drug stories when he himself has mostly had drug experiences that were 'real fuckin' positive'. Here he puts his finger on the absurdity – of all the drug-taking experiences that happen in the world the news only focuses on the most tragic or misconceived. We can see how the routine has been worked through as a response to a series of questions. Chiefly: What's absurd about it? What would solve it? How would I love things to be? He begins by establishing a typical LSD story where a young man on acid jumped out of a building because he thought he could fly. He asks the audience, 'Who are these morons they're finding?' And he expresses no remorse on his death, saying, 'Fuck him, he's an idiot.'

His next question is why the man who thought he could fly ... didn't take off from the ground? Then there's a moment of *personification* where he observes that you don't see ducks lining up to catch elevators before they take off. Then he celebrates that the world has 'just lost a moron'. The comedy here is fuelled by his attitude, and how it contrasts with the mainstream consensus version of events.

Next is a 'how he'd love things to be' bit. This is a reversal of the familiar story where he posits 'a positive LSD story' and argues that it would be newsworthy. Then he goes into an *act-out* which is a *transposition* of esoteric thinking into a mainstream news report. These two things that are totally incongruous are brought together as he parodies the straight, authoritative newsreader reporting on a young man on acid realizing that 'we are all one consciousness experiencing itself subjectively, there is no such thing as death and life is only a dream'. Then he punctures this with the *bathetic* closing line: 'Here's Tom with the weather.'

Questioning the world and yourself is at the heart of stand-up writing. Questions can work for both finding the comic angle in the first place and also for getting more out of an existing idea. And, coming up with questions is easier than coming up with funny ideas! It's then a case of answering the questions in a playful, open-minded way. You're keeping an eye out for the odd gem that goes somewhere.

Pat Welsh also had a student, who while she was an attractive, pleasant young woman, also expressed a lot of negativity (there's a fruitful failing): 'She doesn't hide her negative emotions. I know that from being around her for three years! And I said "That's your shtick. If you're miserable or impatient, we all know it!" I was trying to get her to present that on stage. Comedy is largely the things we don't want people to know about us! It's finding that thing and giving them the license to reveal it.'

Then Pat looks for a subject they might talk about: 'You're asking "What's unusual about them?" This student, she's just twenty-one, and she's engaged. That's unusual. Most students are still playing around, or at least that's the stereotype. So, we started with that. Then [to construct a routine] I often use your comedic structure: set-up/reveal/escalation/payoff.' The set-up gives the audience the necessary information and the context, then the comic idea is revealed, the absurdity or incongruity of it is escalated and the routine is capped off with a payoff (see Chapter 8). 'Set-up: I'm engaged. Reveal: I'm emotional. Escalation: How does he put up with me? Then you need to find the "payoff."'

The set-up, although it's providing information, often will also have jokes in it. In looking for a potential laugh in the set-up, Pat gave her an example: '"So I'm engaged. And that shouldn't come as a surprise. Well, look at me." She's attractive, and she can play high status.' In response to Pat's suggestion, she then wrote an opening line that Pat shared with Tony Allen and me. We discussed what she had written:

**Pat Welsh**   She's actually written, 'Why wouldn't he want me? I've got great tits, a nice arse and I swallow.'

**Chris Head**   Well … the rhythm is 'a three'.

**Pat Welsh**   Yes, she knows the structure, but I ask: Is the 'swallow' bit degrading or empowering? My sensitivity is informed by having gone to university with feminists. But post-feminists might say, 'I do [swallow] and why should I hide it? I do it when I want to.'

**Tony Allen**   The whole thing about it [your comedic persona] being extensions of yourself, it makes you responsible for what you're saying. That's how I used to argue with people being racist, sexist, homophobic and stuff. I don't care if it's a joke. It's offensive. If I'm trying to understand who you are, then you're 'offensive'.

**Pat Welsh**   Is it offensive? What does it say about her?

**Tony Allen**   It's a male understanding of her. It's her adopting a male voice to say it.

**Pat Welsh**   Or is it her manipulating the man?

**Chris Head**   She could make the first two: 'I'm loving/ I'm intelligent' and the third: 'I swallow.' That would have more impact.

**Tony Allen**  That's right, [as it stands] you're already put off by the first two, and the last one just compounds it. Although that is Bill Hicks's joke structure: heavy, heavy, even fucking heavier!

**Chris Head**  She could do the line, then add an afterthought: 'Yeah, but once I've got the wedding ring, I'll stop swallowing.'

**Tony Allen**  Or even better, 'I'm intelligent, I'm sensitive, I swallow. That's not true. I'm not intelligent and sensitive.'

**Chris Head**  So, that way, first of all, the audience think: This is someone who 'swallows'. Then she says, 'That's not true' and the audience thinks: 'Oh she doesn't.' Then just when the audience believe that they've got her, she flips it again: 'Yes I do.'

**Tony Allen**  Then you don't know where you are. What she is then is 'playful and tricksy'.

**Chris Head**  Right. A more engaging persona than 'offensive'.

**Tony Allen**  There are so many different ways of doing that material and you come out of it differently each way.

**Pat Welsh**  She's going to be very pleased when I go back and she finds you've written the bit for her.

# What do you love?

So often in stand-up the starting point is what annoys you or what winds you up. Why else might you be drawn to write about something? In my stand-up courses recently, I've instead asked people, 'What do you love?' It's such a good starting point, it pours out of you, and it's immediately engaging too. And what you see and discover is that within things you love, of course, there are things that annoy you or disappoint you or are absurd in some way. And *that's* the funny stuff.

Samantha Baines is an actor and a club comic noted for her wordplay. She's an *explorer jester*. For her festival shows she uses science, a subject she loves, and she finds the humour by keeping

an eye out for anything incongruous or absurd and then asking
questions and speculating:

> I like finding out interesting things about the world and then
> writing jokes on the back of that. I call it investigative comedy!
> When I started writing I was just wandering the streets searching
> for inspiration or chatting with friends and thinking, 'Oh, is there
> a joke there?' Whereas now I start with something I'm interested
> in. [For example] I read that a building block of particles is called
> a quark. I thought about the word: sounds a bit like 'quack'.
> But why would 'quack' be said as 'quark'? Then I came up with
> a joke, 'Turns out quark is a building block of particles – not
> just a posh duck.' Then I do this posh duck impression where
> I ask for caviar on rye bread. [An act-out; see Chapter 10.] It
> starts with an interesting bit of information and then [through
> asking and playfully answering questions] it goes silly. My new
> show is about lost women of science, who are not celebrated
> as they should be. As I'm reading and researching about them,
> phrases spring out. For example, Sally Ride, who is the first
> American woman in space, she went to space for seven days
> and the engineers at NASA asked her if a hundred tampons
> were enough. Which is obviously ridiculous and I spun off from
> that. First, I thought, 'How many tampons is that a day? About
> 15.' And I wondered about the process of putting them in and
> taking them out and then said, 'Did they think she was a tampon
> machine gun?' Then I do a sort of machine gun tampon action
> [where she is firing them out!]. Then I thought about the moon
> cup which ironically doesn't work in space because liquids fly
> off. Then I thought about liquids flying off and being caught
> out when you're on your period and you don't have anything.
> And so, what would the International Space Station look like?
> A Jackson Pollock. Then I found out they tied all the ends of the
> tampons together so they wouldn't float away from each other. I
> wondered what that would look like. Currently, I say, 'Every time
> she grabbed for a tampon she looked like the old man in *Up* with
> the balloons.' But I think there's something else there because it
> almost looks like a sea creature.

Here we see the question-and-answer nature of developing a
stand-up routine. In stand-up writing, we are asking questions and

coming up with *playful* answers: playing dumb. Ask any question you like, but instead of giving the reasonable, sensible or factual answer, instead you play around with surprising, ridiculous and inappropriate ones. This process wouldn't have happened in one go. Samantha would have worked on it on and off and ideas would have occurred to her at all sorts of random times. An effective writing process will take you back and forth between unconscious creativity and conscious crafting. Ideas emerge from the subconscious so you can't force them. All you can do is ask the questions and then be alert to ideas popping up.

I opened the book by discussing the collaborative nature of stand-up and that very much applies here. You don't need to answer all your questions yourself! Oliver Double discussed how in new material nights and preview shows 'the comedian will go, "I'm writing a routine about X, what's a good reference for X?" Then people put their suggestions in. I've seen Stu Goldsmith doing that. He'll do a Q&A where he'll state to the audience, "I'm trying this new bit," and then if something doesn't particularly work, he'll ask them, "Why didn't that work, or what word can I put in there?"'

In a work-in-progress show at The Stand at the Edinburgh Fringe 2016, I saw Daniel Kitson tell the audience that he was trying to figure out a bit of material. He explained to the audience that he'd recently bought a table and from that point, despite having paid for and received it, Google was continuously showing him adverts for tables. His thought was: *Google thinks it's so sophisticated, but it's so stupid that even though I've got the table in my house and I can't possibly need another, it's showing me adverts for tables.* It was already getting laughs of recognition. We recognized the absurdity. And then he asked the audience, 'What must Google think I'm doing? Why do they think I need all these tables?' Someone in the audience shouted out, 'They think you're opening a restaurant!' Kitson said, 'It's too obvious. We need a situation where I'd need loads of tables but it's not as obvious as a restaurant.' Then a guy at the back shouted out: 'Snooker hall!' and Kitson replied, 'That's brilliant. Snooker hall, thanks mate.' Then he went to his notebook and wrote it down.

Now, let's see if we can write some material right here in the book using this process. For my work in comedy I often catch trains, so let's begin with the basic question: What's absurd about trains?

In the UK anyway, it could be their constant lateness. Yesterday I caught a train that was twenty minutes late. Everyone, whether in a stand-up or a social context, attempts to find funniness through exaggeration (effectively asking the question: How could this be worse?). Exaggerating this, I could say two hours late. Or how about twenty hours late? Or I could push it further and make it two *weeks* late. What are the implications of this? I'd need to set up camp on the platform, get supplies, light a fire. This is the beginning of an *incongruous transposition* of the world of camping into the world of train stations. (See Chapter 7 for more on transpositions and incongruity.)

An idea is starting to emerge here. Maybe two weeks late is an exaggeration sweet spot. Twenty *years* late is probably going to be too much for most comics, but it could be done. It's about knowing how far to go. What about two hundred years? Some of these wilder exaggerations could work if you are a surreal-world comic. Let's try it. My instinct, by the way, is to be more specific than the round 'two-hundred' figure so I am going to make it 209 years late:

> The train was so late, it was ridiculous. I thought at first it was meant to come at 18.09. Turns out it was meant to come *in* 1809. It was 209 years late! We were waiting for this bloody steam locomotive. I was on the platform with a young mother, an office worker and Lord Byron. I just wanted to get home. He wanted to get to Greece to support their nineteenth-century revolution against the Turks.

Here we find a short surrealist routine springing out of a real-life experience. This brings us to the question of style (see Chapter 4). From the same starting point of the late train, a very different routine might have been written that closely observed the reality of the situation and through epitomizing key absurdities hit a different exaggeration sweet-spot.

# Stand-up levels

Here's a final question for you. What levels does your stand-up material operate on? One of the great things about stand-up is that it can embrace everything: gross scatological stuff can happen alongside linguistic wordplay and opinions; even big ideas about the meaning of life. Many comics, however, restrict themselves to the same narrow range. I have co-developed a dramaturgical tool where you analyse the levels the act operates on and invite them to try others. Here it is:

1   base level: sex, scatology and the body;
2   emotional level: interpersonal dynamics and relationships;
3   desire level: hungers, yearnings and egos;
4   heart level: personal disclosures and revelations;
5   mind level: language, analysis and opinions;
6   philosophical level: ideas, theories and thoughts;
7   sacred level: spirituality and transcendence.

Let's take 'food' as a topic. At at the first level you'd be discussing sex games with food, excretion, maybe being overweight or underweight. That kind of thing. At the second level, it could be how your mother fed you or dining out on dates. At the third it might be indulging, dieting or Instagramming your meals. The fourth level would be honestly sharing and connecting with the audience on personal issues around food. At level five you might talk about the politics of school dinners or fair trade food. As this is also the level of language, food puns would come here! The sixth level might be vegetarianism or the ethics of food production. And finally, you might consider fasting as a spiritual practice or the Hindu serving of blessed food as 'prasad'. The style with which you treat these topics of course would be dependent on your persona and comic world, but most comics can hit most levels in their own way. (I define the 'comic world' as the totality of the comedian's style, tone, persona and biography.)

I gave this list to an act once, and he now uses it as a checklist for his Edinburgh shows. He aims to be hitting every level in a show, which is setting a high bar. I feel Bill Hicks for example ranges across all these levels. How about George Carlin, Lenny Bruce, Joan Rivers or Richard Pryor? Where do you gravitate towards on this spectrum? Can you expand your comedy to encompass levels on which you don't currently operate?

# 3

# How directors and stand-ups work together

At the time of writing I am directing five shows for the Edinburgh Fringe 2017. In conventional theatre, the idea of directing five shows at once would not compute. A directing process for a play might be three weeks of full days in a rehearsal room (longer if you have the luxury). It's a full-time job for all involved. In a stand-up context, I'm able to spin the plates of five shows simultaneously as the process is spread out over a far longer period and involves many short bursts of contact rather than a sustained focus over a period of weeks.

When I directed Katia Kvinge's 2016 Edinburgh Fringe and touring show *Squirrel* the rehearsal process consisted of weekly sessions in a pub in Clapham Common over three months, augmented by me watching videos of previews. So that's a directing process over several months, but it can be even longer. For example, Phil Nichol is currently directing musical comic Jonny Awsum. Phil told me, 'We've been working for a couple of years on the idea. We met first on the South Bank for an afternoon, for free. He said, "I've got five ideas." I said number four was the one he should do. I feel completely involved in his show [Jonny Awsum's Edinburgh 2017 show is *Honey, I Promised the Kid*], because he wants to do something different.'

This is a directing process that has been going on for two years! Whether it's weeks, months or even years, how does the process unfold? Phil Whelans has recently directed an Edinburgh stand-up show for the excellent Stephen Carlin. He described the process:

Stephen's agent suggested he have a director. We met in cafés a lot and round at my flat – we talked, and then I went to see previews. Often comics don't have time to spend in a rehearsal room, so they want me to go and see previews and give them notes. It's how stand-ups like to work a lot of the time; trying jokes out in tiny chunks and building something. I worked on a show for a comic a couple of years ago, and I think I should almost have insisted that we do at least a fortnight of Monday-to-Fridays in a rehearsal room, like with a play. But stand-ups who just write something down on the back of a cigarette packet and try it out in a gig, working a show like you would work a play is quite counter-intuitive.

## Stand-up dramaturgy

What is the stand-up director doing during this potentially lengthy and often intermittent process? Where I am involved with a show from the outset (rather than being brought in later in the process), I am initially acting as dramaturg; drawing out themes and ideas, perhaps helping give the show a title and helping craft the blurb for the programme.

Of our work together on *Squirrel,* Katia recalled, 'The discipline of meeting each week was really helpful. Just having those three hours and *we're working on this now* – that really helped. It's having someone to bounce ideas off, isn't it? And someone keeping you accountable as well.'

Dec Munro commented, 'Compared to theatrical direction, I think you might be more of a dramaturg. And part of your job is saying: "In two weeks, get me the script." That's not conventional directing, but [it's important] to be able to set people absolute deadlines, and they believe that you mean it. They can't buy their way out of it by charming you.' Ahir Shah discussed working with a director on his stand-up shows:

> There's a lot less of 'you should be holding yourself this way' or 'try using this arm' or whatever. The physicality of it tends not to be the central thing. It's more dramaturgical, being able to tease out wider themes, or '*This* is where emotionally your audience are at this stage but where you want them to be is *here*.' The director can also see an act's blind spots. For the last few years, I've worked with the director Adam Brace. The usefulness of

having that exterior view will vary from comic to comic because every comic has their own flaws. Quite often, the nature of your flaws is such that even if you can recognize that they exist, they're not things that you can do anything about yourself. Because you just naturally fall into those habits. I am very much a person who will overwrite or not know when to get in and get out of a bit quickly enough. That's the sort of thing that having someone on the outside of it can be really useful for.

# Material

Another key aspect of the stand-up director's role is helping select, rework and develop material. Kate Smurthwaite discussed how she helps an act decide what material to include in a show:

> It's very easy, especially when you're doing your first hour, to say, 'Here's every joke I've ever written, let's put it all together', rather than taking a step back and asking, 'What do I want to achieve here?' That's one of the things that a director can probably tell you. They may also be able to see your work in a way that you don't. [When Kate works with an act on a show], We start with a pile of blank bits of paper and then end up with a table covered in notes: Here's some bits which are definitely going in, here's the maybe subjects and here's the "I'd like to talk about this but it seems a bit serious" pile. Then you keep the other stuff that might fill a gap. Then there will be stuff *not* to include. For example, there might be a very old hat joke. Sure, it gets a laugh, but does it get a laugh that is uniquely *you* and moves the story forward? Or are we just trying to think of a way to stop the audience from being miserable for an hour? They're quite different goals. Over an hour-long show you have to say something.

In addition to being a sounding board and helping to select and develop material, a director can at times almost become a co-writer. Mr Cee commented, 'Sometimes you can give a gift: "*This is the line.*" Some people graciously accept the gift! But it's always the act's decision whether they accept it or not.' Where the director is themselves a stand-up there can sometimes be a conflict of interest. Phil Whelans recalled, 'In a couple of cases I ended up writing chunks of their show, which feels more than my job should be. And in one case I wrote something for them and thought, "I'd rather have that for myself."'

Kate Smurthwaite avoids this dilemma by picking shows to direct that are different from her own work: 'It would be weird to direct somebody whose show was left-wing, feminist, political commentary because if I've had any good ideas about that, I'm sorry, they don't leave these four walls! I do end up writing quite a lot of jokes for people, which is fine. As far as I'm concerned, if they've hired me to direct them, whatever I write on their time is theirs. You're on the same team trying to make a great show.'

In my own case, in common with other specialist directors like Paul Byrne, the fact that I don't perform myself allows me to be free with ideas, jokes and suggestions. But equally you can simply ask good questions to try and take them to a new idea. And often I find even when I do make a suggestion they adapt it and make it their own, or it sparks off their own idea. Also, I often have a sense of the kind of idea that would fit and I don't articulate it fully. I just hint at it, leaving them to fill in the details.

How does a director or a coach talk to an act when some material is simply not working? Oliver Double discussed the kind of situation in a classroom where a student has tried something in front of their peers, but it bombed. His approach to handling the situation also applies to stand-ups in gigs and shows:

> The first thing I'll say is, 'How did you feel that went?' If they reply 'It was fine' then you can press them a bit, because normally they know. If they then say 'Oh, I was disappointed' then you ask 'What was your thinking?' And if they then initiate a discussion – 'Well, I was trying to do this' – then you can throw suggestions at them. It's about objectivity. If there's no laugh there, it's objective. I'm reading the audience. It's not saying 'That was rubbish.' It may be that I didn't understand what they were trying to do, and probably the audience didn't either. Then you can ask 'What was the point you were trying to make?' And then when they explain it you can say 'Okay, how can we make that work?'

I find the key to talking about material to a comic (of whatever level) is to talk about it in a distanced, objective way. It's '*the* idea' not 'your idea'. It becomes this third thing we are both looking at. Oliver Double agreed:

> It's about being able to step back from the thing, and say: 'All right, what can we do with it?' You create this distance from it, and then it becomes easier for you to step back from it, and look at it together. It's about being objective: 'I think that's a funnier joke than the laugh it got. It got a little laugh, but I think we can get a big laugh out of that. What can we do?' It changes it. It's not like you're saying, 'I didn't like it', it's more: 'Well it didn't work. Why?' And actually, now even when someone is doing something good, I ask: 'How can it be better?'

# Structure

As a stand-up director, I work closely on structure and this is a central aspect of the director's role. For example, with Samantha Baines's show about unjustly forgotten women in science, when I started working on it with her she had her material on US astronaut Sally Ride (see Chapter 2) at the start because it was the strongest. However, I felt it needed to go at the end because the ideas and images were so outlandish (much more so than anything else she had) that it would not leave the show anywhere to build to.

Dec Munro, director of Sofie Hagen's show *Bubblewrap* told me, 'My input was mostly supporting her huge talent and ability. I think my biggest role was to help Sofie structure her show to achieve what she wanted. That said, some of it was simple staging stuff. We looked at crowd work together, and there are some reveals in the show that needed to be carefully managed, so road testing them repeatedly in front of a bunch of audiences was useful but the structuring was the key part.'

And John Gordillo gave me an example of working with a comic on structure: 'I had a wonderful experience working with Charmian Hughes, who had a lovely show about being 60 [*Soixante Mirth: 2012*], and meeting her previous selves at different times of her life. I really gave her that structuring, and she brought material. It was just a lovely collaboration because she was open to it. You don't force that on anyone. There's a lovely interplay between her silliness and my structure. Then obviously she's taken it on and it's totally her own.' And Kate Smurthwaite told me of a show she wrote and performed as a stand-up, where the outside eye of the director brought a neat structural device to it:

> Sam Miller directed *My Professional Opinion* and it had a lovely structural joke. It was his idea from seeing it at a distance. The show was all about how we form opinions. At one point, I say, 'Don't just trust the internet.' So, we went to the website WikiHow and we found an article about how to form an opinion. We decided we'd use that as a basis for the show. It didn't work very well with the structure we had, so we rewrote that *How to Form an Opinion* article on WikiHow to put in into the order that I wanted for my show! In the show, I said we're using something I found on the net. And then at the end there was a reveal where I show at the bottom of the page it names the author. And it turned out that I'd written it. Sometimes there's really lovely structural jokes like that.

## Previews and performances

Most of the early meetings for me happen in cafés and then when the show needs to be on its feet, we can meet in a pub or rehearsal room, bits of it can be tried out in clubs and then there are preview shows. Some comics like this time of standing up and performing in front of the director – and some directors insist on it – but others feel they can't perform without an audience. Either way, getting the work in front of audiences is the key step and seeing and feeding back on the multiple preview shows, billed as work in progress, is an essential part of the director's role. I tend to watch previews on video (at least until towards the end of the process) which has the advantage of being able to discuss footage with the act.

That way I can point out things that worked that they didn't particularly think about and say, 'Try and do that again.' Or, 'I think maybe next time, try this slight adjustment or take a slightly bigger pause.' Or, 'That was great there where you lifted your head up.' It's a process of making them aware of things that are working and things that aren't working, so that it's more likely to work next time in the moment but without being an explicit instruction or a command to execute something in a particular way. Simon

McBurney discussed with me the importance of getting the work in front of audiences:

> The key that I've taken away from making things which were essentially about trying to make people laugh – and I still do it with my own pieces – is that you only find out what happens when you're in front of people. You have to stand up and do it and then find out. You have to get the vehicle and give it a bit of gas. See if it runs and then take the motherfucker back into the garage, take it all apart again. Change the carburettor because it doesn't really work at all. There's an aspect of stand-up that's just extraordinarily technical. Where *that* simply doesn't work. But then you put that *there* and suddenly it all works. And after all that, sometimes you realize, that all that fiddling and changing simply leads you back to where you started. It's as simple as falling over; failing. Failing again. But, you hope, failing better.

When a show reaches the Edinburgh Fringe, Phil Nichol, like me, will be there for the tech. For stand-up shows, this tends to be minimal, but can increasingly involve the use of projection and other elements like live music. Phil said, 'I'll set the lights and the sound levels, pick the pre-show music and help make decisions. Then I'll see a preview in Edinburgh. [The first shows of an Edinburgh run are preview shows.] Then I'll leave you alone during the first week. If I get a chance, I'll come see it at another point before the end of the festival.' In my case, not having my own show to perform, I attend the first two or three shows and then after the first week, my work is done, and the show is up and running. I remain available for queries through the run and would be very happy to return should an award be in the offing.

# Beyond the Fringe

Many Edinburgh shows then go off on tour, and some stand-up shows just tour on the back of a TV profile without ever having been to a festival. Do these acts work with a director? Geoff Whiting told me, 'Gary Delaney and Jarred Christmas have just been touring and they didn't have a director. I think those kinds of acts might be well advised to have a director for a tour show, because a tour is as important as an Edinburgh show. If people will buy tickets based on their name, they should really make sure that the show is spot on, and I think a director can help them do that.'

A common approach with touring stand-up shows is for acts to do 'two forty-fives', two stand-up sets of three-quarters of an hour. Geoff Whiting added: 'Take Henning Wehn for example. He's doing the Guernsey comedy festival for me. He's doing two 45-minute sets. It's the main event of the festival, and it's a 700-seat room. I think he's doing that without a director. In Edinburgh, he might be playing a room with 200 people, for less time, yet then he would have a director.'

Clearly then there are established TV acts touring shows that don't have a director. They will, however, have other 'outside eyes'. Oliver Double for instance writes about the wives of Alexei Sayle and Omid Djalili giving invaluable input to their shows.[1] And there *are* big-name touring and stadium acts which engage the services of a director. John Gordillo has directed Eddie Izzard and also Michael McIntyre.

> In Michael's case, he just needed someone to be there in the room with him and to talk it through. He'll say 'I don't know what's funnier. Tell me what's funnier.' Yes, absolutely, you can feed him with jokes and ideas, but I didn't direct Michael in the sense of saying 'This is what you could be doing.' I've never worked with anybody better than him. I've never worked with anybody who's faster at processing the world into material and who has such an instinct and a gift. However, I think he's at his best when he's doing work in progress, because there's something about his vulnerability, about the flow of him as he's piecing it together and riffing on his ideas, which is already more advanced than most of us can do.

# A change of direction

Stand-up coach and director Logan Murray has directed acts at all levels, including Milton Jones in his 2006 show *Caught in a Rabbit's Headlights*. Milton's motivation to work with a director was his desire to showcase more than what he had become known for:

> He had very specific intent. He had some very, very funny visuals – he had a big box of props he brought out. It was completely

different from the '*I think the police should have special powers
... like flight and x-ray vision*' material that he usually did. He
wanted to remind everybody what he was capable of. My job
was to laugh and to stage it. Just being an outside eye. He had
me doubled up: I thought 'Well, the one thing I know is that I'm
quite average, so if that makes *me* laugh, the chances are it's
going to make everyone else laugh.'

John Gordillo's work directing Mark Steel also came about because
the comic wanted to do something new. John sees this as a particular
moment when an established comic can benefit from working
with a director: 'Mark Steel came to me and said "I want to do a
different kind of show. It's all about my dad and finding out that I
was adopted." And that's somebody who is obviously an incredibly
functional comic, who wants to apply his skills in a different area,
and wants to find a narrative.'

Simon McBurney discussed with me how a director can help a
comic find a new direction:

> Stand-up is extraordinarily exposing and, with any comic, once
> they reach a certain stage in their career, there's a vulnerability
> because ... what do you do next? You're Lenny Henry and
> not only has everyone seen what you do, they want you to do
> it *again*. The same characters. The ones you did twenty years
> previously. With Dawn [French] and Jennifer [Saunders] there
> were people coming [to the show] who wanted Dawn in a dog
> collar and Jennifer holding a glass of gin. Rowan Atkinson's Mr
> Bean was what people wanted, but he wanted something else.
> And, I suppose, the object of having a director, of employing me,
> was to have somebody who would provoke a change of route.
> I was never part of their pasts, I came from a completely other
> tradition, although the world of comedy was where I started.
> When I was very, very, very young – yeah right – I performed at
> the opening night of the Comedy Store [in 1979 above a strip
> club in Soho] along with such luminaries as Arnold Brown,
> Alexei Sayle and Rik Mayall. I had a double act with – wait for it
> – Sandi Toksvig. But that was long ago; a story for another time.
> But I guess Lenny, Dawn, Jennifer, Rowan – and Hamish McColl
> and Sean Foley with whom I also worked when they began to
> form their company The Right Size – they all wanted to grow in

another direction. And looked for someone who would wield a chainsaw with impunity. Cut some branches to allow others to grow. And to the best of my ability I attempted to do that.

## Stand-up versus theatre directing

A director of actors could decide: 'I want to stage a production of a theatrical monologue. I need an actor. I will audition, cast someone and then they will fulfil my creative vision.' It is inconceivable for a stand-up director to proceed in this fashion. If the acting director's work is top down, stand-up is bottom up – it begins with the act. At the time of writing, I am working as a director on Samantha Baines's 2017 Edinburgh show *1 Woman, a High-Flyer and a Flat Bottom* at the Pleasance Courtyard. Renowned for her wordplay, she also draws on science for her festival shows. She said of these hour-long shows:

> Because I'm an actor, I think it's really important to have a director. Obviously, in acting, I always have one. I know lots of comedians now *do* have directors, but it's weird with stand-up because it's so personal, and you're playing *you*. And with acting, if the director tells me to do something I do it, because they hired me to do a job. It's their vision that you're helping to create. Whereas with stand-up, it's *my* vision: If the director tells me to do something, I will choose whether or not to do it.

This is radically different from film, theatre and TV directing. In stand-up, the power lies with the performer: the director is serving *them*. Mr Cee discussed this dynamic where the final say is on the side of the comic:

> For example, you say to the act 'The reason you're not getting the laughter you expected is because the punch word is in the wrong place.' Because we teach comedy, we know the structure of it. The punch word should be at the end of the sentence. And they'll say: 'No, but that's how I talk. That's how I would say it.' But it's not a question of how you would say it, it's how to say it to get the biggest impact! But the beauty of performing stand-up comedy is that *you* make the ultimate decision on *what* you're

going to deliver and *how* you're going to deliver it. No matter who is giving you the advice, it's your call at the end of the day. I used to get upset with it: 'The punch word is in the wrong place, man!' The comedian will say: 'Look, Cee, is the audience laughing?' 'Yes, they're laughing, but they should be laughing harder!' Now as a director I just have to accept it.

One further significant difference between stand-up directing and directing actors is this: The stand-up might have *multiple directors*. Kate Smurthwaite again: 'Some people come to me as a director and then *also* go to somebody else, and I don't think that's a problem. I don't have an attitude of "*I* am the director. No joke can be put in without my say so."' This is another consequence of the stand-up (or their agent) recruiting the director, rather than the director recruiting the actor. With Samantha Baines's 2017 Edinburgh show I am one of a number of outside eyes: 'This year I'm getting a few different people to look at it and give me notes. I think when you work with one specific director, as a team you can get really wrapped up in what you're doing, and sometimes it's useful to get someone in who's never seen it before. It's useful trying it in front of different directors. And weirdly what's different from acting is the fact that you don't take all of it. Just the bits that really strike a chord with you.'

So, if they don't get the final say, they may only be one of a number of directors and are often anonymous, why do stand-up directors do it? According to Phil Nichol, 'I just enjoy the process. I've got lots of time for helping people get the best out of the material they have.' I agree with that sentiment, and for myself (having started as a writer/performer) I find I get far more satisfaction as a facilitator who is able to work on an extraordinary range of shows from autobiographical stand-up, to one-liners, to character acts, to musical comics, to impressionists, to science comedy; a far broader range of work than I'd ever be involved with if left to my own devices.

# ACT 2

# Writing and performing stand-up

# 4

# The interplay between writing and performance

When we discuss stand-up writing, in common with, say, novel or play writing, there are many different *styles* that one might actually write in. The director and stand-up comedian need to have a clear sense of the comic style that they are operating in, so that the material they develop is consistent in tone and approach. Indeed, I find that one of the pleasures of directing comics is moving across styles. What style are you? Or what style is the act standing in front of you? Acts do have a consistent style. We can see straight away that Bill Burr and Steven Wright have very different styles and that Amy Schumer's style is far more akin to Burr's than Wright's. Meanwhile, Seinfeld's comic style is different again and Steven Wright is operating in his own parallel universe. His kind of comedy is often termed *surreal,* so I have borrowed some other words from the world of art to try and capture the range of comedic styles.

Here are the comic styles that I identify: *realist, sketch, cartoon* and *surreal.* Each is getting further removed from reality. *Realists* share their very personal shames, fears, embarrassments and failings openly. The material is complex and emotionally truthful. For example, Tig Notaro is famous for talking about her mother's death, a serious breakup and breast cancer. Other *realists* include Amy Schumer, Richard Pryor and Billy Connolly in that they are sharing the unflattering truths of their lives.

*Sketch comics* remain anchored in the everyday world we all recognize, but it isn't so personally exposing. Examples include Jerry Seinfeld, Sarah Millican, Jack Dee ... and probably the majority of comedians. *Cartoonists* are often playful and silly, sometimes dark and can also be downright incongruous. Not much, if anything, of the stand-up's real life is revealed. Examples include Demetri Martin, Milton Jones and Emo Philips.

Finally, with the *surrealists* we are now in dream world where all laws and expectations break down. Anything can happen. It's full of impossibilities and strange transpositions (see Chapter 7). *Surrealist* examples include Eddie Izzard, Noel Fielding and Ross Noble.

When I set the four styles out visually, I do as four points on a (usually very scrappy) circle. When I'm working with a comic I like to identify with them the area they tend to occupy. Figure 1 is a comic who fundamentally employs *sketch* as their style but does at times reveal something more honest about themselves.

Represented as a circle, *surrealists* might also shade back around into *realists*. I feel Maria Bamford is here, around the north-west corner; a fertile real/surreal meeting point. This model can be diagnostic of a comic whose style is not defined. If you have a comic whose style comes out as in Figure 2 the task is to narrow it down. There are simply no established comics who range across styles like this. (However rule-breaking mavericks like Hans Teeuwen or Jordan Brookes, who deliberately switch styles, at times come close!)[1]

As we consider stand-up writing in this section of the book remember, with the exception of something like *puns* which are very much identified with *cartoonists,* few techniques are aligned with a specific style. For example, *personification* is used by the highly realist Richard Pryor *and* by the wilfully surreal Eddie Izzard. And

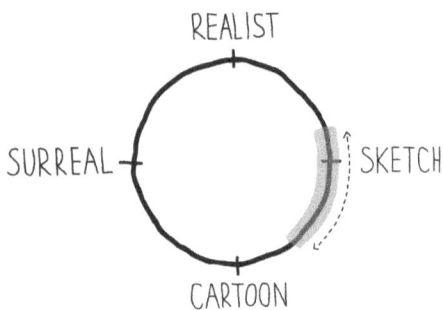

**FIGURE 1**

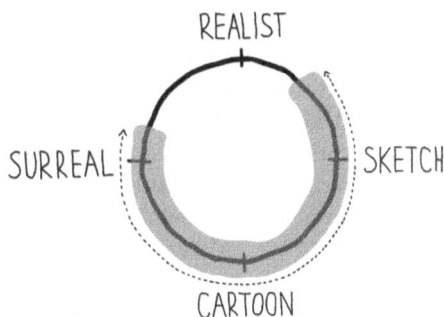

**FIGURE 2**

basic fundamentals like set-up/payoff and misdirection cut across all styles.

# Stand-up writing and improvisation

Explaining my work to someone at a party recently, I was met with the response: 'But isn't it all improvised?' The short answer is 'No', followed by me slipping away to the vol-au-vents. The longer answer is that stand-ups exist on a spectrum. At one end, you have the very carefully worded and crafted one-liner jokes of the likes of Milton Jones, Stewart Francis or Steven Wright. These jokes are dependent upon precise wording, pacing and delivery and are largely impossible to improvise, at least in any quantity. (Although Milton Jones, for example, will go on stage having worked out a joke carefully but then leaving the precise wording to be discovered in the moment.[2])

At the opposite extreme, you have someone like Ross Noble who will do a lot of ad-libbing. He'll have prepared material too, but his shifting between that and improvising is so seamless that, unless you know the act intimately, it is tough to distinguish between the two. In between improvisation and crafted one-liners are the great bulk of comedians who have written material they are delivering pretty much as planned, but have wriggle room to change the odd bit on the fly and to work the room.

And even the act of actually writing stand-up is a very open and free activity. You might do it on a laptop, or in a notebook, or by recording voice notes or even compose it mostly in your head. Comics also write on stage. As well as finding the best wording or timing on stage, you may also discover a line, a tangent or a whole routine and that goes back into the writing. And comics will often go on with a loose idea and improvise capturing the result, refining it and going again in front of another audience until it settles down into some material – without ever becoming fixed. So, when I refer to 'writing' stand-up, there are all these possible ways of pulling it together.

However you do it, you are looking to create the feeling that you are talking to the audience, not reciting a piece of writing – even when you are. You are aiming to achieve the naturalness and freshness of being funny socially. In fact, there is a strong feeling of a social occasion about stand-up in a way there doesn't tend to be with other kinds of performance. The performance style can be easy, natural and interactive like a good conversation; there is an in-the-moment responsiveness to what's going on in the surrounding environment – intimate, personal stuff can be shared – and both conversation and stand-up are about banter, jokes and laughing at shared references.

# Responding to the live environment

Barry Ferns is a highly regarded compère and co-founder of Angel Comedy in London. He's a *caregiver creator*. When we spoke, Barry reflected on what makes a good night: 'Storytelling informs my understanding of a gig. We live in a very individualistic age and a lot of people think the person on stage is giving the comedy and is the big "I am" of the situation. My understanding is this is not that case at all. The person that has the microphone is the *conduit* through which everybody has the comedy experience. It's a trick of perspective that one person is making it happen. *Everybody* there makes that experience of being in a gig.' So, what is the role of the person on stage? Barry replied, 'It's like being Pan, the playful spirit in the room, whose energy other people can contact within themselves.'

He told me that he sees emceeing a comedy night as akin to hosting a dinner party: 'There are things in a dinner party you have to mention; where the toilets are, that the potatoes are overcooked, that Terry's going to be late because they're having parking problems or whatever.' Just as the host of a comedy night needs to address any issues. Barry continued:

> As an emcee, like a party host, the conversation will come out in a certain way as dictated by your persona. If you're an anxious party host then it's going to be a party where everyone's freaked, keen to please you and tell you how nice the potatoes are. But if you're a relaxed party host they might take the piss out of the potatoes. And at the same time, while you wouldn't write out a set list if you're hosting a dinner party, you might be aware that something funny happened in New York last week when you were there and that your guests might enjoy that story. You've got fifteen different stories that you could potentially tell but, as with the audience in a comedy gig, other people are talking, and you want to interact so stories may or may not come up. As an *act*, you're a lot more focused on what you want to say. You're driving the conversation. You're very much a guest of the dinner party. You're going to be less interested in making sure everybody gets on and more interested in asserting your standpoint.

While it's more literally a conversation the emcee is having with the audience, as an act it can really help get the tone right if you too think of stand-up as a conversation. Admittedly, it's a very one-sided conversation and (as an act) you're doing the vast majority of the talking (which would be very annoying socially), but it's a conversation nevertheless. The keys are that it is happening in the present moment, in the same space as the audience, and with the particular people who are there, which is radically different to an actor performing a character's speech in a play that imaginatively is happening in a different time and space. For example, the actor is in the royal palace at Elsinore in the Middle Ages, while the audience is in a theatre in the twenty-first century. When you are doing stand-up, the audience is in that room, on that night, and so are you. An actor in a conventional play won't come on as Hamlet and say: 'It's great to be in this lovely old West End theatre', but a stand-up absolutely could.

Actors also have to ignore whatever is happening in the room, such as people looking at their phones, talking or falling asleep. We can see how unusual it is in this context because when an actor does pick up on someone's behaviour in the audience, it makes the newspapers! However, even classical theatre is beginning to be influenced by the present-moment responsiveness of stand-up with, for example, Andrew Scott in his 2017 Hamlet performance saying he really wanted to speak directly to the audience and 'not pretend they're not there'. He discussed audience members potentially sneezing or laughing too loudly, or how when heavy rain falls it's audible in the Harold Pinter Theatre. All of this kind of thing he wanted to acknowledge to make it feel live and direct.[3]

You can also prepare recovery lines, which is a line you have ready to say if a gag falls flat. A standard one is 'That sounded funny in my head' and one I devised is (said to the emcee or organizer, who I have randomly named here) 'Okay Kenny, release the tumbleweeds.' This 'working the room' is central to stand-up because stand-up is live. Another kind of prepared line is the put-down or comeback to a heckle. There is a large shared archive of such lines that comics all draw on. And, of course, people write their own or simply ad-lib in response too. Whether it's prepared or more spontaneous, if you are talking to the audience without reference to the context, how they are reacting or what's happening in the room, then they might as well be watching you on YouTube.

# Stand-up writing and spontaneous speech

Newer acts often find there is a conflict between getting the material right and having a connection with the audience. Geoff Whiting recalled, 'Sarah Millican, at the start, delivered her act like a monologue. When she did her second gig, I remember it distinctly, I saw how many notes she had. She said to me, "This is the whole act. I've memorized it word for word. If I'm heckled, I have just to keep going because if I stop, I can't remember where I am in my script." So that's a very good example of someone who couldn't do the set *and* talk to the audience. Later on, of course, she cracked it, but it is quite a problem for a lot of acts in the beginning.'

It can really help to keep your act alive and natural sounding if you remember you are writing *speech* when you write stand-up. Write it like a character's speech in a film and not like a nicely written story or newspaper column. Then, at least, it will sound like you are talking spontaneously, rather than remembering a text. Here's an example stand-up snippet that I wrote some years ago for a class where the comic is ranting about last weekend's

TV talent show. (There'll usually be one that the routine can be adjusted to fit ...) I wrote it when my daughter was two. She's eight now so there is a real danger that she might actually read it:

> Did you see [insert name of TV show] at the weekend? I think humiliating delusional people who can't sing on national TV is like taking infant school kids and laughing at them because they can't talk properly – on national TV. Oh, hold on a minute, Chris Tarrant has done that already. That's one for the oldies in the audience. Do you remember that show? *Kids Say the Funniest Things*? Well I've got news for you – no, they don't. I've got a two-year-old. That show should have been called, *Children Say The Most Whiney Demanding Annoying Things – And Then Throw Their Dinner On The Floor*. Okay, a bit too angry there. It's the sleepless nights. So, no that's not fair. They do have their sweet moments. Like I'm sure Saddam Hussein did. I can see a few of you without toddlers thinking that's a mad comparison. It's not. They're little dictators. Do you know our nickname for her? Pol Potty.

Make it seem like you are discovering the stuff as you go. Make it feel like a thought process. (Notice, too, the short statements.) If the *writing* isn't like this, it'll be hard for the *performance* to come off as such. The key here is that you are not writing something to be *read,* you are writing something to be *said.* So, write in a conversational style that connects with the audience. Let's break down this kind of writing and work on a routine that begins:

> This weekend was our wedding anniversary!

Of course, it doesn't matter whether it was or not, it could have been six months ago. Saying it was 'at the weekend' simply makes it seem natural that you're talking about it. If there's no reaction from the audience you could say:

> Thanks for the congratulations.

If they *do* happen to clap, then it doesn't get triggered. Hence this is a prepared line waiting to be *triggered* by a particular response (or in this case non-response) from the audience. You can increase the likelihood that the first line *won't* get a reaction – and so give you the non-response you are after – by saying it in a deadpan way. After that you might then invite a different response by repeating in an upbeat way: '*I said, this weekend was our wedding anniversary!!*' And then when they do respond: 'Nope, too little too late.' Another example of a triggered reaction is Gary Delaney saying to his audience after they laugh at an early joke in a set: 'Good, well done. I put that one in as a test and you've passed.' Cleverly making them want to show they have got his clever gags by laughing! (Put-downs that comics have ready to go in response to heckles are also examples of triggered lines.)

Let's continue writing this routine, using a conversational style and working the room. Regarding getting this tone, this conversational feel, I often ask comedians I am working with: 'Would you say that socially?' I am not referring here to the content – stand-up gives you licence to talk about all kinds of things you might not readily broach off stage – but I mean would you *phrase it like that* socially? Furthermore, in writing stand-up, you're always looking to switch or flip tone or content. Here is an opportunity:

> [upbeat] This weekend was our wedding anniversary! [downbeat] It does help if you remember it, doesn't it?

Now I recognize I'm getting into familiar territory, *the man* forgetting the anniversary, but one way round this problem is to voice this objection in the material by working in some *metacomedy*, which is about the process of comedy, it's self-referential:

> Nah, I'm joking! Of course, I remembered it! [pause] And there's no way I'd forget after last year. [mime pain in crotch] And I thought she wanted more kids.

Here there is a *mime* to communicate the idea – it's all implied. You give the audience enough to work it out. And if it were a woman delivering this bit she could have fun with the stereotype that we *expect* the *man* to forget the wedding anniversary:

> [upbeat] This weekend was our wedding anniversary! [downbeat] It does help if you remember it, doesn't it? It's usually the guy who forgets though, right? [upbeat again] Challenging gender stereotypes!

Some material is starting to emerge from the basic idea of the anniversary, and all of these switches are potential laugh points. And we have built crowd work *into the routine* itself to make it sound chatty, natural and interactive. You can include questions, address the audience and even reflect on the delivery of your own act *in the script*. Oliver Double gave me an example of this in action:

> I did that with a bit of a material I used when compèring student shows. There's an Indian restaurant in my home town where they were advertising an Elvis theme night. I just thought that was really funny and the poster said, 'songs by Elvis Presley and songs he may have done had he lived!' Then what I thought was, 'Well, there's got to be a bunch of like Elvis/Indian themed dishes.' Then I wrote down as many Elvis/Indian dish puns as I could, chose the best ones, and then worked out a sequence. Then I thought, 'The problem with this is people sometimes groan at puns.' So, after the first one, I added in, 'Look, that's a pun, and I've got loads more of these, and I'm going to do them whatever you do. You can either agree we all think puns are really funny and we're going to enjoy it, or you can just sit there miserable for the next two minutes.'

These kinds of insertions will make it seem more fresh, dynamic and chatty when you come to deliver it. Stand-up dies when you are just trotting out a piece of writing with no regard for who is there and how they are responding. So, bring all of this live, responsive stuff into the 'script'. The material and working the room can be intertwined all the way through the process, rather than 'working the room' being something you ad-lib on stage if you're in the mood. This approach doesn't in any way rule out ad-libbing since, on the contrary, it sets you up to do so since your whole act is now outward looking and discursive.

# Reading the room

As stand-ups become more experienced, they become able to pick and choose which material to include in their set based upon the situation they find themselves in – this is reading the room and can also happen on the fly during the performance. For instance, I also often advise acts to have a bail-out point in routines, which is where you identify a moment in the routine and you give yourself two options at that moment. For example: If they laugh *at this point*, I will do the following ninety seconds of material building on that gag. If they don't, I will skip it and jump to the next bit.

Kate Smurthwaite, when working as a stand-up, finds, 'There are nights when you get there and you think, "With this lot I'm just going to have to do very accessible stuff that doesn't require much concentration." Because often in a club, the audience might be quite drunk.' But some comics refuse to change their material according to the audience they are performing to, which might be for strongly-held political reasons. They don't want to compromise their views even though *this* particular audience won't share their politics and so they may struggle in the gig (the absolute exemplar of this was Bill Hicks's extraordinary 'flying saucer tour' where he unrelentingly sticks with his usual act with audiences who are antithetical to his worldview). Or they might hold a strong feeling of artistic integrity which they are not willing to compromise. These views are valid.

At the same time, returning to Barry's dinner party analogy, it's like saying, 'I will converse in exactly the same way whoever the guests are. No matter who it is; my mates, my partner's parents, my daughter's friends. I won't change.' As a compère, Geoff Whiting has seen acts fail who haven't adjusted to their context. For example, 'I've seen people come back from Edinburgh who've just been nominated for the comedy award, who then die on their arse in a twenty-minutes club set. They're doing twenty minutes out of their hour, and people are thinking "there aren't enough jokes." Unless you're in an arts centre with a very particular vibe, they don't want the Edinburgh-type stuff.'

# Keeping material alive

Even once you have arrived at some material that mostly works (whether it was carefully written in Word or derived from a series of performances), don't then consider the job done. Stand-up writing is never a finished product like the text of a play. As Logan Murray observed when we spoke, 'Even if you think something is finished, it really never is. You're out gigging and six months later, it's grown and developed. You as the author write something and then you as the performer almost have to think, "Someone wrote this, how can I make this work?"'

Logan described to me how comics can feel too precious of their material. 'They think: "It made an audience laugh once, so I must deliver it exactly the same way again and again." I'm sure we both know comics who gave up because they just gave robotic clockwork performances.' And many comics I have worked with have said of a piece of material: 'This was killer when I first did it, but now it's really not working so well anymore.' I always think that they have held it too close and are trying to replicate something rather than letting it live again. Logan went on:

> It's particularly prevalent with some people when they rant. We're all good at improvising a rant if the audience gives us the right energy and then the next day you think, 'Oh that rant killed it, so I'll do it again.' But you're not actually in the moment anymore. You're constantly looking back, thinking, 'How did I do it last night?' Whatever people write, it's just a blueprint for the real art which is the performance in front of the crowd. You might think, 'I've nailed that, I know it works.' Then you find yourself at a gig and all you do is raise an eyebrow or put a downward inflexion on one particular word, and suddenly it gets a much better reaction. I think the bits of your brain where our ideas come from, are arguably much cleverer than the conscious brain. If you play with the medium and how you deliver stuff, then it will change. Then like a jazz musician doing variations on a theme night after night, you hit on something you weren't planning to do.

How can all this possibly be directed? I typically offer these thoughts: Remember that you are not delivering a monologue by Harold Pinter where you have to be faithful to every word. The 'script' is merely a blueprint for what you have to say, so don't feel you need to reproduce it exactly. Over time your freer version of the material will often settle into something consistent anyway, but will always have that openness and spontaneity. You can plan for some ad-libbing, leaving certain bits more open and freshly wording them each time on stage – as long as you know what you're doing with it and why it's funny. Don't 'overwrite' and, in fact, what you get down as 'writing' might just be bullet points. This interplay between writing and performance is where stand-up comes alive.

To create a freer feel to your set that can allow for improvisation and interaction with the audience, with the material it can be a good idea to distinguish between elements, where you

- definitely want to use the wording you've 'written' and no other;
- need to be precise with the kinds of words and the rhythm, but the exact wording is not so key – you just need to get the gist of the meaning;
- can deliberately leave things open until the exact wording or the path through it emerges on stage.

You can mix and match all these approaches. For example, you might take the second approach for the set-up of a comic idea or joke, and the first approach for the payoff. This creates a more spontaneous feel to the performance. And finally, Stewart Lee told *Mustard* magazine that after he had children, people said to him that his stuff seemed much looser and improvised: 'And I have to pretend that's an artistic decision rather than being down to the fact there isn't the time to sit at home and piece it all together. You have to work it out on stage, which ends up giving it a much more conversational feel.'[4]

# 5

# Writing jokes:

# Afterthoughts and beforethoughts

Jimmy Carr once set himself the task of writing the shortest possible joke and he came up with a two-word joke ... but he got in trouble for it (over two words!). The two words were: 'Dwarf shortage.' Despite its brevity, this is *set-up/payoff*. The first word is the set-up and the second the payoff. Two words are as short as you can go with purely verbal jokes. You can't have a one-word joke. Or at least if the one word gets a laugh then it would have been set up by something non-verbal. For example, if a vicar walks onto the stage in a comedy club (and I have coached a genuine stand-up vicar), in full regalia, gets to the microphone and says 'Fuck!' ... and it gets a laugh ... it's still set-up/payoff. Set-up: 'A vicar walks up to the microphone.' Payoff: 'Fuck!' (My stand-up vicar doesn't swear, by the way.)

Every time you say or do something that triggers a laugh that's the payoff, whatever preceded it was the set-up. Set-up/payoff is the fundamental comic rhythm. Take for example the old slapstick slipping on a banana skin gag: the set-up is the person walking towards the banana skin, which we the audience see and they don't (dramatic irony). Then they slip on it: payoff. How much we laugh will partly be determined by how amusing the slip is – abruptness will help; comedy thrives on sudden transitions, be they visual or verbal. But crucially the set-up is doing a lot of work in preparing the ground for the funniness; a neutral person slipping may have some amusement value. But what if he were a banker on his phone bragging about a deal and then he slips?

In this chapter, we are looking at joke writing through the medium of the one-liner, the smallest unit of comedy. Then in Chapter 9 we will see how many of these self-same techniques apply to larger pieces of comedy like a routine or story. First, terminology. In comedy, people often talk about the *set-up/punch* rhythm. As you will have noted by now, I mostly use the word 'payoff' rather than 'punch' to designate a line, word or action that gets a laugh. 'Punch' very definitely implies an ending and the word 'punchline' refers purely to verbal jokes. When I use 'payoff' I am referring to any moment that gets a laugh – it could be verbal, physical, silence even – and at *any* point in a performance, routine, story or joke, not simply the climactic moment. In fact, comedy, whether it's stand-up, clowning or sketch tends to be constructed as a series of set-ups and payoffs, leading to a climactic payoff.

Even musical comedy follows this structure. I direct Steve Whiteley's musical, stand-up character act, Wisebowm. Steve's act is a mix of spoken material and rhymes and raps with a musical backing. Part of my early directing work with Steve was getting the gags to be more consistent and frequent in the rhymes. I have found with a lot of newer musical acts that the songs are not joke-focused enough. They are amusing and often clever, but do not have enough moments when the audience will laugh out loud. Steve said, 'I always wanted it to rhyme well, and I wanted to do clever wordplay. The comedy came secondary. Then over time that changed because it doesn't matter how clever something sounds, or how good you think it is lyrically, if it doesn't get laughs, it doesn't work.'

The remedy is a simple one: You need to look at the songs in terms of their set-up/payoffs. So, line one of a verse is a set-up, line two is a payoff, then line three is a set-up, line four is a payoff and so on through the piece. As with spoken stand-up, there can be smaller laughs along the way to the next big one *which has to be at the end of the verse or chorus*. Another issue is that with a normal song the chorus simply repeats. Ideally, in a comedy song the writer will find a way of varying the chorus so that it has a surprise each time in order to get a laugh. Steve went on, 'That has massively adjusted my focus; working with the set-up and then the payoff as you would a gag, then always having a gag in the final line. That structure has been really helpful.'

To return to terminology, after the payoff you might have a *topper*. Geoff Whiting described it to me as: 'Putting a second punchline after a gag [without a further set-up]. Often, you'll say "That's a great line and you got a topper on it." Comics also use the word "tag." To tag a line on another line.' In British usage it's similar to, but not quite the same as *topper*. 'Sometimes it will mean they're going to tag something on, a little bit of information or something else. It may not literally be another punchline. Where the topper is *always* another punchline and they really do mean something they think will get a big laugh.' But in the United States the two words seem to be interchangeable. US stand-up coach Greg Dean writes in his glossary of stand-up terms that *topper* is 'an antiquated term referring to a joke playing off a previous joke; same as tag'.[1] Oliver Double commented, 'The language changes over time, and it changes geographically as well, like the American things are slightly different from British.'

US comics routinely use the word *bit* for a routine, or a section of a routine, but that is not so common in the UK. Geoff Whiting again: 'UK comics would use "routine" 90 per cent of the time and if not then "piece." And you'll also often hear the word *banker* used for their best gags.' These are the ones that work near-as-dammit every time and can be relied upon to get a laugh. 'People would say "Start with a banker" or "Finish with a banker." Or if they have a bad gig they'll say, "I threw in a couple of bankers and it still didn't work."'

## Callbacks

Another unarguably established term is the *callback*, which is used in the United Kingdom and the United States. (Also known as 'reincorporation'.) A callback is unexpectedly bringing back something from earlier and re-contextualizing it. Geoff commented: '"Callback" is probably the most common phrase in comedy.' Samantha Baines observed: 'They're very satisfying for an audience. They like being in on the joke. But obviously they only work if you've done the joke you're calling back to! Lots of times you see comedians doing a callback to a joke that they haven't done. And if you know their set, you can say to them afterwards, "You didn't do the initial joke, that's why the audience didn't laugh at the callback."'

Callbacks can be particularly satisfying the longer the gap is, so you've got real scope in an hour-long show to do quite a long-range callback. Samantha went on, 'The problem I have as I'm editing [my new festival show] is that I've written callbacks and then cut out the original joke because it wasn't strong enough. But then the callback is strong. Do I leave it in just for the callback?' Geoff added, 'Comics also talk about burning material: If they do material on Live at the Apollo or something else on TV, then they can't use it in the clubs or on tour and they'll say they've "burned it."'

## *Misdirection*

Let's look at a joke that has been thoroughly burned by being part of Dave's Funniest Joke of the Fringe award, an annual tradition at the Edinburgh Festival Fringe. (With thanks for Dave's kind permission to quote jokes from the award lists.)[2] This gag is from Jack Whitehall:

> I'm sure wherever my dad is; he's looking down on us. He's not dead, just very condescending.

It's a *misdirection* joke which works with the ambiguity of the phrase 'looking down on us' which the joke reveals both means 'condescending' and is a euphemism for someone being dead. Geoff Whiting believes the word *misdirection* was adopted relatively recently: 'People used to use another phrase, *pull-back-and-reveal*. That was the expression that was used when I started. But now 99 per cent say *misdirection*.' I asked Geoff if he hears *rug-pull* being used for the same technique: 'Yes, but I think that's transatlantic. I don't hear many British comedians say that.' Here's a joke, from Mark Watson, that also uses misdirection:

> Always leave them wanting more, my uncle used to say to me. Which is why he lost his job in disaster relief.

When we hear the set-up, we assume the uncle was in showbiz and he's talking about audiences to his nephew, the stand-up comedian. There is a whole series of these 'my uncle used to say' jokes. Peter

Kay had an earlier one where the uncle, who'd habitually say 'Always fight fire with fire', lost his job in the fire brigade. Stewart Lee (sending up this kind of joke writing) had his 'uncle' who said 'Never judge a book by its cover' being sacked from the book cover design of the year award. He adds, 'See I can write jokes, I just choose not to'. This is an example of metacomedy where he self-referentially refers to the process.

## *Rule of three*

The Mark Watson joke is in a *rule-of-three* rhythm: 'Always leave them wanting more/My uncle used to say to me/Which is why he lost his job in disaster relief.' A three-part rhythm is common for a one-liner – so yes, a *one*-liner might actually be three lines. It's also found in many other areas; for example in political speeches, in phrases like 'education, education, education'. Geoff Whiting hears the term *rule of three* used a lot: 'Yes, "rule of three" is standard and used all the time. It is sometimes used to mean there are three lines [or parts] in a gag and the third line is the punch line. It is also commonly used to mean that if you have a gag such as "sex in strange places" you name three (no more/no less) places. It applies to all such gags where a "list" of examples is used.' Yet another manifestation of the rule of three is defined by Tony Allen in his book *Attitude* as 'establish, reinforce, surprise'.[3] For example: Monday, Tuesday, Banana. Here's a rule-of-three gag from Annie McGrath that does this:

> Don't you hate it when people assume you're rich because you sound posh and went to private school and have loads of money?

The reason it's three is that two is the minimum you need to establish a pattern and comedy is always economical; you simply don't need 'Monday, Tuesday, Wednesday, Banana' – and 'Monday Banana' is not enough. Whether it's three or more, whenever you have a list in your material (of whatever length), always add an absurd one to the end. A new stand-up I was working with talked about the lottery and had a straight list of things people buy with their winnings:

> When people win the lottery they buy a house, a yacht, a helicopter.

Keeping the rule of three in mind and adding an absurd one at the end brings in an extra possible laugh, and then a second potential laugh here when you react to the audience's reaction:

> When people win the lottery they buy a house, a yacht … ten thousand Jaffa cakes. [looks at audience] Okay, that's just my dream then.

Two extra potential laughs just from switching a straight list to one with an absurd item on the end.

# Found set-ups and afterthoughts

'Looking down on us', 'leave them wanting more', 'fight fire with fire': I think of the starting phrase of these kinds of jokes as a *found set-up*. The phrase becomes a joke by taking it literally, making it personal, putting it into a context and adding a payoff.

I have adapted the idea of *found set-ups* from Marcel Duchamp's 'readymades' where he took everyday objects he'd found in the world and, by adding something, turned them into art – the most famous being *Fountain*, the urinal that he signed 'R. Mutt' and entered into an art exhibition in France in 1917. The origins of these readymades were in 1915 when Duchamp bought a snow shovel from a hardware store on which he wrote, 'In advance of a broken arm.' Essentially, Duchamp had found objects in the world that the maker had not intended to be art, but then by adding his own touch he turned them into art objects.[4] We could say that the original, found object was the set-up and Duchamp's intervention was the payoff. Here's another example from Tom Parry of a punchline being added to a *found set-up*, in this case a saying:

> Red sky at night: shepherd's delight. Blue sky at night: day.

Try looking up sayings, proverbs or adages and adding your own comment that undermines it in some way or turns it on its head. Here's a venerable one from W. C. Fields:

> Start every day off with a smile – and get it over with.

And here's a rather more recent one subverting a related proverb from Paul F. Taylor:

> Money can't buy you happiness? Well, check this out, I bought myself a Happy Meal.

And this one from Stuart Mitchell adds a bit of context before the phrase and also leaves us to work out the rest:

> Why is it old people say 'there's no place like home', yet when you put them in one ... .

Logan Murray usefully describes these kinds of interpolated payoffs as *afterthoughts* and I have adopted his term.[5] As an exercise, google 'inspirational quotes', treat the quotes as found set-ups and try adding afterthoughts. Here's an example of the kind of thing you might end up with – from Oscar Wilde no less:

> Always forgive your enemies; nothing annoys them so much.

You can also interrupt an edifying or improving quote half way and change how it finishes. Another from Mr Wilde:

> Anyone who lives within their means ... suffers from a lack of imagination.

The ellipsis indicates where the original phrase was broken away from and an alternative ending inserted. Here's a gag from Nish Kumar that also interrupts a found set-up:

> My mum's so pessimistic, that if there was an Olympics for pessimism she wouldn't fancy her chances.

This is based around a familiar phrasing: 'If there was an Olympics for *x* so-and-so would win gold.' Here though the regular phrase is interrupted and ended differently. It is set up in such a way that we have an expectation of where it's going ... then it goes somewhere else: *misdirection*. And it's in the first person, and personal: 'my mum'. First-person perspective is the most common voice used for stand-up and is a hallmark of modern acts; the personal perspective.

It used to be the case that comics would say things like: '*This bloke walked into a bar.*' Nowadays it'd be '*I walked into a bar*' or at least '*I saw this bloke walk into a bar.*'

Second-person perspective is another common register in stand-up: '*So, you walk into the bar.*' This tends to be used for observational material where the comic is sure the audience will share the experience. If you are using the third person in stand-up – '*they go into the bar*' – you are talking about a group you are not in, or a category of person who is not in the room. (This can be potentially problematic if you are 'kicking down' to a weaker group, but it all depends on your attitude and intention.) Here is a gag from Hannibal Burress where he has added an afterthought to a found set-up; this time a conversational cliché and it's in the third person:

> People say 'I'm taking it one day at a time.' You know what? So is everybody. That's how time works.

Note how the use of a question – 'You know what?' – makes it conversational and also tees up the payoff. The rhythm is disrupted without that question. One way of writing jokes then is to start with a phrase that the world has offered to you, the found set-up, and then to add your own afterthought as we have seen in these examples.

# Found payoffs and beforethoughts

You can also start with a found payoff! This isn't to say that the joke was handed to you on a plate. In its original context, the phrase was not intended to be funny but can become so by adding a carefully worded set-up. To illustrate this, here's a winning gag from the Dave's Funniest Joke of the Fringe award, this time from 2014. It's by Tim Vine who is a regular on the Dave list:

> I've decided to sell my hoover. Well, it was just collecting dust.

First, note that the joke is in the first person, personal. This makes the joke feel more modern and less of a *joke-book* joke. A more old-fashioned version of the joke might begin: 'Why did the man sell his hoover?' But having said that, if there is anyone who doesn't care about sounding old fashioned (indeed who positively revels in it) it's Tim Vine.

How would you set about writing this kind of joke? This time the key is to start at the end. This joke works on taking the figure of speech, an idiom ('just collecting dust'), literally and then *working backwards* from this found payoff to write a set-up. This is essentially the opposite of an afterthought, which, for neatness, I'm calling a *beforethought*. I'm not sure this term will catch on, but, then again, it's now in print and it'll look all authoritative in the index so you never know. A lot of wordplay jokes are written backwards – the comic notices the potential in a word or phrase and then constructs the set-up. This requires more of a mental leap than adding afterthoughts. The working forwards joke writing method echoes the way jokes come up socially:

Person A says something (the unwitting set-up)

Person B *straight after* adds a quip (the afterthought).

Simple. Socially this would be mind-bending:

Person A says something (the unwitting payoff)

Person B says he's just realized that if he had said a phrase *before* Person A spoke it would turn what Person A had just said into a quip (the beforethought).

Do you follow that? I'm not sure Person A would – and Person B here would probably not get many laughs socially. But he would be able to write jokes. Here's another example of this kind of thinking, this time from Masai Graham:

My dad has suggested that I register for a donor card. He's a man after my own heart.

Again, the joke begins with taking the phrase literally – 'a man after my own heart' – and adding a *beforethought*. Another approach is to construct a joke around a *homophone*. A homophone is where one sound has two different meanings. For example, this incredibly tight one from Simon Munnery:

Clowns divorce: custardy battle.

Here is a one-liner joke from Rob Auton that is also based on an idiom *and* exploits a homophone (as created by the branding industry):

> I heard a rumour that Cadbury is bringing out an oriental chocolate bar. Could be a Chinese Wispa.

Note how he is at pains not to have the word 'Chinese' in the set-up. This is an important point with one-liners – ideally no key word from the payoff should be in the set-up. Sometimes you can get away with it, but often it's the kiss of death for a gag. Look how clunky it would be if it were like this: 'I heard a rumour that Cadbury is bringing out a Chinese chocolate bar. Could be a Chinese Wispa.' Comedians work hard on finding synonyms and roundabout ways of putting things in order to avoid having key words from the payoff in the set-up. Interestingly, Rob Auton is not *at all* a one-liner act. He conceives high-concept stand-up shows that stretch the form. Rob discusses the genesis of the joke:

> When I was working in the art supplies shop, someone [mentioned] Chinese whispers. I thought 'Oh yes, there is also a chocolate bar called a Wispa.' When I went up to Edinburgh in 2013 I said it at a ten-minute spot but it wasn't in my *Sky Show* because it wasn't about the sky and I couldn't find a way of shoehorning it in. One morning I got a call on my mobile saying that my joke had been voted as the 'Dave Funniest Joke of the Fringe'. I was proud of my *Sky Show* and suddenly I was going to get a lot of exposure for a joke that I wasn't 100 per cent convinced was brilliant. There was no way I was going to turn it down though. And I got a lot of people on Twitter getting in touch saying that they had written the joke. What I think they meant to say was they had written the joke *as well*. I bet loads of people have written that joke.[6]

You can try out adding beforethoughts using an online dictionary of idioms. I have just googled 'idioms' and picked out the phrase 'against the clock', which of course ordinarily means under time pressure. I can't hear a homophone in the phrase, so let's try taking it literally. The first question is: How could you be *literally* against a clock? Well, leaning against it is one way. And as with Rob Auton's joke where he avoids the word 'Chinese' in the set-up, here you have to find a way of saying 'clock' without using the actual word. It struck me that naming a famous clock would do the trick which suggested Big Ben. (Yes, I do know that Big Ben is technically the bell.) Then I tried to think of a situation where you could both be against the clock literally and figuratively, I wrote a beforethought and a joke (such as it is) was born:

> I was rushing to catch a tube in Westminster, got tired and leaned against Big Ben. But I had to move on as I was against the clock.

Not a joke that would get into the Dave shortlist, but you can see the process. With Rob Auton's joke the word 'rumour' in the set-up does the job of making both meanings operate in the payoff (it's a Chinese Wispa *and* it might be a Chinese whisper), here the word 'rushing' brings both meanings to the payoff (leaning against the clock *and* being under time pressure). When both meanings are operating in the payoff it can be more satisfying (but no guarantee of hilarity – it is perhaps necessary but not sufficient). So, what's the secret? Well, there's native wit and a facility for this kind of wordplay of course. But more simply it's practice and quantity. The real secret of joke writing is this: If you want ten really good jokes write one hundred.

Writing these kinds of jokes is often a case of going fishing for raw materials. You can use the process with any phrase: sayings, lyrics, titles. Let's try film titles. Pick one where there is an ambiguity or a double meaning or a homophone and then work backwards to come up with a set-up. For example, 'Last Tango in Paris'. 'Tango' could be referring to a dance or a soft drink (it's a homophone). Then with a beforethought:

> 'Did you see that film about the great French soft drinks shortage? Last Tango in Paris.' Then you could add: 'That's what it's about, right?'

I think this is an improvement on the 'against the clock' gag, but the problem with using idioms or very obvious phrases as a starting point, as Rob Auton found, is that other people will have probably hit upon the same idea. Indeed, Dave's winning joke for 2017 was written by Ken Cheng and, as Twitter quickly pointed out, it turned out to have been written many times before in various versions.

I'm not a fan of the new pound coin, but then again, I hate all change.

Nevertheless, it is still possible to hit on a novel one. You can increase your chances by working with more specialized or unusual phrases, as long as they are shared by the audience. It's not just words however that can serve as starting points to work backwards from. Oliver Double recalled a Milton Jones joke. He said it to me: '"I was walking down the street the other day and I saw a small dead baby ghost. Although, I think about it now, it might have been a handkerchief." What you've done there is you see the handkerchief, probably on the road, and his thought is, "Well, it kind of looks a bit like a baby ghost." That's the incongruity [see Chapter 7] and then the work is finding the form that that line comes out in.' And that's adding a beforethought. Let's close with a joke from Zoe Lyons, *a rebel jester,* that won the 2008 Dave's Funniest Joke of the Fringe award:

I went on a girl's night out recently. The invitation said 'dress to kill'. I went as Rose West.

This joke exhibits pretty much all the main aspects of stand-up joke writing that we have discussed. The joke is in three parts, the *rule of three*, but it can also be looked at in terms of the *set-up/ payoff* structure. The first two parts are the set-up and the third is the payoff. The joke is in the first person, which is a hallmark of modern stand-up jokes. It has been worked on to get it incredibly economical. It's hard to see how you could take a word out without affecting it. You could lose the word 'recently' and it would still make sense; that word however has a job to do. It's making the joke sound conversational and current. The words that trigger the laugh are at the end. The writing of this joke begins with noticing that the idiomatic phrase, 'dress to kill' – which the audience will take to mean 'to dress up stunningly' – also has a literal meaning of dressing up to commit a murder. So, it's had an afterthought added.

I asked Zoe about her writing process: 'I don't tend to write things out long form. I have ideas that I jot down and then I'll try them on stage. It's both terrifying and thrilling to do new stuff for the first time on stage. Sometimes you can hit the joke straight away but other times it can take a while to make it funny. It could be a matter of setting it up differently, or just changing one word and it starts to get laughs. You're constantly learning doing this job; learning how to write better material and how to present an idea in a better way.'

Crucially, this joke makes the audience do some work. The majority of jokes require the audience to make a mental leap; they have to 'get it'. Here is the joke without any work required of the audience: 'I went on a girl's night out recently. The invitation said "dress to kill." I took this literally and dressed up as a murderer.' To go from this to a joke, the comic would need to work out how to *imply* that they're dressed as a killer so that the audience have some work to do. There's not an obvious 'killer's outfit', in the way there is with a cartoon burglar say; stripy top/swag bag. How about a specific killer? In Zoe Lyons's case, it needs to be a woman. And so, for the UK anyway, Rose West fits the bill. Note that the exact reference could change over time or according to which culture the joke was told in. If you didn't get the joke and have been mystified by the last few paragraphs, now you know why.

And finally, the joke suits the teller's persona. Zoe Lyons being a high-status in-your-face kind of person that you could imagine being this outrageous. It could in theory be delivered by someone low status and clueless as an embarrassing admission of a dreadful misunderstanding. But not here. I asked Zoe about her persona: 'My persona is just a slightly exaggerated version of the off-stage self. I just ramp up the physicality of my character. I probably appear more confident on stage than I actually am. I think I have learnt to be more myself on stage over the years. As a new act, I certainly had a constant mantra of "please like me, please like me" when I was on stage. That has gone now, which I think frees you up as a comic (but seriously ... please like me!).'

# 6

# Re-writing jokes:

# To fix them, improve them and suit the teller

Let's move on to consider the re-writing of jokes. In the previous chapter we explored joke writing techniques and approaches. To illustrate the principles, we examined finished and indeed award-winning jokes. But focusing on these is to miss out on the crucial middle phase between idea and finished article: the tinkering phase. We'll explore it through the work of Richard Lindesay and Samantha Baines, both of whom I work with and both of whom are known as craftspeople of the well-constructed gag.

## Fixing a joke

New Zealand comic Richard Lindesay is an *innocent jester* and he has something of an otherworldly air about him, and specializes in offbeat one-liners, not unlike a young, Antipodean Milton Jones. I have been working as a director with Richard for around four years. We began working together via Skype when he was doing unpaid open spots in Australia. He's now based in the UK and we have graduated to working together in person, and Richard has graduated to being a busy paid act on the UK comedy circuit and beyond. Let's start with a gag of Richard's that is conceptual rather than language based.[1] Originally it went like this:

> I eat a lot of pumpkin seeds. Not because I like them but because I hate pumpkins.

He observed:

> This was one where even though they weren't really laughing I thought, no this is good, I'm just not explaining it right. So, I thought I've got to add some words to give them time to cotton on to what's going on. I find that if I don't have a few words at the start before I say the important thing, they sometimes miss it. So, I ended up putting it after another joke where I've talked about not eating many fruit and vegetables so it leads into it. Then padding it with: 'I don't eat a lot of vegetables but I DO eat A LOT of pumpkin seeds.' And then I pause and I say: 'Not because I like them, or because they're healthy.' And in that little bounce there, I see them catching up. They're like: 'What?!' They've got time to wonder. Then I say: 'But because I hate pumpkins.' Most of them get it now. And I follow it up with: 'And I believe in solving life's problems before they get out of hand.' Then everyone gets it. I have a tag as well that I will use if I have time: 'The same thing applies to jelly babies. Everyone likes them which is why you never see jelly adults.'

The problem wasn't that the idea wasn't funny, rather it was that the audience weren't understanding what was meant. Many times, I've found comedians about to cut out a joke because it's 'not working' but in fact the idea was *potentially* funny it just wasn't understood by the audience. And often, as here, the solution may well lie largely in paying attention to the set-up, making sure the audience have all the information they need before you reveal the comic idea. Sometimes the opposite is the case too – the audience have too much irrelevant and distracting information, so then it's about identifying what's relevant and what isn't, and then cutting. And, of course, sometimes it really isn't funny.

# Re-writing a joke

Here's a misdirection gag from Mark Smith, which is an afterthought to (what sounds like) a found set-up:

> Apparently 1 in 3 Britons are conceived in an IKEA bed which is mad because those places are really well lit.[2]

The original statistic was of course referring to beds that had been bought and taken home; that is our natural assumption when we hear the statement. The wording here is ambiguous and Smith deliberately misunderstands the statistic. Notice too how he makes us work out the implication of what he has said. The phrase 'those places are really well lit' is a clever, indirect way of making us realize what he means. I worked with stand-up Richard Lindesay to develop this kind of statistic-based gag that, when I first heard it, went like this:

> The average daily energy intake for a man is 2500 calories which makes me above average.

This is an *afterthought* gag; Richard has added his own take on a statistic that he found in the world: 'This gag simply points out the ambiguity around whether "above average" is good or not, and plays on the fact that I'm a bit overweight.' While it had got a laugh, we felt it could be improved to get more from the audience. Here's Richard's first rewrite:

> I heard that the average daily energy intake for a man is 2500 calories. It's nice to be above average.

Richard observed, 'This now breaks the gag into a two-part structure making the punchline stand out a little more.' This feels clearer and punchier and indeed works better. The full stop marks the shift from a set-up to a payoff. A big pause here would be too much but a beat could help the rhythm. This version also adds the misunderstanding that Richard thinks that it's positive to be 'above average' and making Richard's attitude about the whole situation positive plays into his lack of self-awareness as a persona. Having found the set-up/payoff structure we drilled down more into the rhythm of the line, adding some words to the payoff:

> I heard that the average daily energy intake for a man is 2500 calories. Not every day you find out you're above average.

Richard commented, 'This version adds some fat before the "above average" punch, which to me feels like it improves the rhythm, and gives the listener some breathing room.' This was an improvement on the second version and worked better. The comic idea has not changed but, by working on the structure, rhythm and attitude, it is enhanced. A final step was to put the joke into a context – a visit to the doctor's – and to shift it into a three-part structure; the *rule of three*:

> My doctor told me that the average daily energy intake for a man is 2500 calories. So that's good. Not every day you find out you're officially above average.

Richard went on, 'adding "so that's good" reinforces the set-up and gets a giggle, and adding "officially" with a small pause afterwards which is a signpost to the punchline and makes it stand out more.' With all this in place the gag worked much better.

Richard began as an act that delivered entirely disconnected one-liners. When we started working together, we looked at putting jokes together into routines and contexts. Richard already had several jokes around doctors and we were able to thread them together into a story about a negative doctor visit. From the perspective of the audience, they may well have thought: *Richard had a bad experience at the doctor's and he was able to find a lot of jokes from that experience.* Whereas the reality was he had several disconnected jokes around doctors that could be reworked to become a routine on the subject. This 'calories' joke found its final form as an end to this routine. In this context:

> My doctor did give me some good news though. He told me that the average daily energy intake for a man is 2500 calories. So that's good. Not every day you find out you're officially above average.

This illustrates how relatively small technical changes can get more out of a joke. I have a useful checklist of things to consider when looking to flesh out the details and the context of a gag. Richard recalled:

> When we first met in London, there were five little things you said that really resonated with me. I was just over from New Zealand, where I had been saying disconnected jokes, and you said: put it in context, add emotion, find the attitude, make it personal and make it motivated. So, I went through all of my material with that in mind, and if something didn't have a context I tried to put it in one. I asked 'What would my emotion be around this', and then I acted that. Then I thought 'What would my attitude be' and I portrayed that. Then I tried to make it personal if I could, with the motivation being the main one. You asked me: 'Why are you saying this?' That changed everything for me, in terms of how I thought about the order, placement and setting of material. I now keep those five things in front of me when I'm trying to put a routine together.

For example, Richard had a joke that went:

> I saw a sign that said thieves may operate in this area. Like they've got permission.

He goes on:

> I started playing with it with those five points in mind, first thinking 'Why am I saying this?' My first iteration was 'I was in a shopping centre and I saw a sign', so at least I was in a place. Then from that I asked 'Why would I notice it?' Then I thought it could be tied in with the fact that I'm new to the country, and I don't understand things. That's making it personal. So, since the audience don't know me, I should say that I'm recently arrived from New Zealand and I'm struggling with the culture. So, I'm giving it a context, making it motivated and making it more personal – making it more of a story. Now I say 'I was in a shopping centre and someone came up to me, grabbed my bag and ran off.' That often gets a bit of a giggle. Then I say that I was about to go after him when I saw the sign: 'Thieves

may operate in this area.' So, it's about me seeing the sign in a certain situation and making a mistake because I'm new here. Now there's also movement in the joke: Somebody is coming up to me, grabbing my bag and running off, so I thought I would make the gestures to reinforce that.

The genesis of that joke was Richard's seeing a sign in real life and noticing its ambiguity. For Richard, 'The way my mind is wired, I see the alternative first before the intended meaning. I always have: I just never used to say it out loud, as I didn't think it would be funny. The ones that work less for me are the ones that I think everyone would misinterpret in that way. The ones that are better are the ones that feel particular to my character.'

## Making a joke suit you

Let's turn to the topic of re-writing a joke so that it fits *you*. Sometimes early versions of a comedian's own material simply doesn't suit them. This could be down to the persona or biography of the comic or the style. I asked Richard if he had a sense of his persona when he started. He said of his early gigs, 'No, not at all. In fact, it came out completely differently from how I thought it would. I practised in a jovial way, but over the first ten or twenty shows I was just distant and staring at the back of the room. It was like a deer-in-headlights. But people liked it! It was a bit of a surprise. One gig there were some pro acts there, and they said: "We really like your character." And I thought: character?! It was just me trying to remember the material.'

So like Jack Dee, Richard stumbled on something that worked for him, which was primarily him performing artlessly, not talking to people, not connecting to the room. There was something about that strange, aloof distance that clicked with his material. A clear example of how your failings can be your strengths: 'Then when I tried not doing it, it stopped working! I just started talking like a normal person and I got nothing. My wife – who comes along and watches a lot of my gigs – she says, you lost your character. Then I realized how important persona is to all of this. Now I find that if I walk on in the right way and I get a bit of a giggle before I even start, then I know I've the character established.'

And there are also the biographical details of the persona: 'When I started working with you, you were talking about painting the world of the character and making it ostensibly autobiographical. Whereas when I was in Australia I was just like, "Here's a bunch of new jokes I've written" and I was all over the place. Without the coherence of the persona and without the ideas joining it just wasn't working consistently.'

Even today we still work on making sure the biography is consistent across the set. For example, in a recent gig at Komedia in Brighton, Richard had one joke where he referred to 'his girlfriend'. And a later joke hinged on him being single. Well, it's one or the other, you can't be both. Or you have to change when one joke happened in relation to the other. Richard said, 'When it came to figuring out what material to use, defining the character put restrictions on me and that helped. It made the decision process miles easier.'

When we first started working together, I watched a video of Richard's gigs and it was evident that his persona thrives on a lack of self-awareness. He doesn't realize how strangely he is coming across. Naturally, the audience know what the game is, and sometimes Richard does acknowledge he is doing jokes, but most of the time it relies on the character not realizing how weird his life is: dramatic irony. Here's another Richard Lindesay joke:

I lost my job at the Samaritans for answering the phone with: 'Okay, shoot.'

This gag is typical of Richard's punchy, absurdist jokes. We suspend our disbelief and allow ourselves to believe that he got a job at the Samaritans and then lost it. The manner of him losing the job fits in with what we, the audience, have learnt about his character; namely that he messes things up in a cheerfully oblivious way. It makes sense that he would lose the job because of this.

In an early direction I gave Richard, I pointed out that the act is about *his* madness. That's what the audience enjoys. And yet some of his jokes at that time were about the madness *of the wider world*. For example, he had a gag about a new design of aeroplane. The joke went like this:

I hear that Boeing and Walkers have got together to make plane-flavoured crisps.

The joke in effect made out Boeing and Walkers to be mad. Given that Richard's act thrives when the world is normal, and *he* is being crazy in it, I suggested he bring this gag into line with that by making it hypothetical. He then produced this rewrite of the joke:

> I like it when companies get together and collaborate on ideas. What I'd like to see is Boeing and Walkers getting together. To make plane-flavoured crisps.

Yes, it is longer, which some would consider a cardinal sin – brevity being the soul of wit – but it's in a neat rule-of-three structure and it is now consistent with his persona and comic world, which is more important than word count. In its original version, it got a reasonable reaction, but when he changed it from Boeing's design to his idea of a fantasy plane he would love, the joke then got a bigger laugh. It played into the craziness of the persona that the audience was already enjoying. I encouraged him to have this in mind when he wrote jokes: to keep the world normal and make him the mad one. This is an essential element of his comic world.

Here's a recent situational joke Richard has been trying recently in his set but that hasn't quite worked. Again, the solution was to rewrite it to fit Richard's comic world:

> I do face painting at the zoo. I paint tiger faces on the kids. I like to take it a step further and paint kids faces on the tiger cubs. Then I like to put them all in together and see if they'll play.

Richard liked this joke: 'But it tends to get a little or not much at all [audience laughter]. I think it's a step too far; it's obvious it's not true.' It might sound strange to be concerned that the audience doesn't believe this is true when of course they also don't think it's literally true that he had a job at the Samaritans. But with the Samaritans gag, they're willing to suspend their disbelief and here they're not. So why not? It's because it doesn't fit with his comic world where everything is normal apart from Richard's behaviour. In the Samaritans joke, the only one who is behaving strangely is Richard and the world responds appropriately: He loses his job.

The zoo gag, however, requires many people and even animals to behave strangely: We have to believe that the zoo keepers would allow him access to the tiger cage, that the cubs (and their parents) would accept him painting their faces and that the zoo keepers and the kids' parents would turn a blind eye to him putting the kids and the tiger cubs in together. And all of that is why it gets less of a laugh! How might you fix this? The easiest way is, again, to make it hypothetical. I put this to Richard, and he responded with:

> I enjoy face painting tiger faces on the kids so much, maybe the next step would be to paint kids faces on the tigers.

Here we also cut 'cubs' to make it punchier and a straight reversal, and we have lost the idea of him putting the kids and tiger cubs in to play together, but I like the simple, tight new version. Richard too liked the quality this one had. It felt, as he put it, 'Like I'm figuring it out on the spot.' And it would get a better reaction as it no longer violates Richard's comic world. As another approach, I then suggested he use the jobs formula that we have previously seen:

> I got fired from my job face painting at the zoo. I enjoyed painting tiger faces on the kids so much I thought I'd try painting kids faces on the tigers.

A key aspect of this version is that he 'tried' to paint kids faces on the tigers which suggests a whole cartoon of his thwarted attempt. I then suggested, that at the end, Richard look at the audience with a *'What?'*, in effect reacting to their laughter with a 'What's wrong with that?': 'Yes it's good to put the joke into a structure I already use: namely "I lost my job ..." It gives it a familiarity. I always like saying "*What?!*" in response to an audience laugh.' We went on to talk about how in Noel Fielding's comic world, for example, it would be fine to assert that he literally painted faces on tiger cubs and then he put them and the kids in to play together. In Fielding's surreal-world comedy, by definition, everything in the world is strange and dreamlike. For example, I recall an early routine of his about all the letters of the alphabet living together in a forest – so painting kids faces onto tiger cubs would be no problem. As for Richard's own more grounded world, where he is the oddball, but everything else is as it should be, Richard observed, 'Yes I've come to realize it's suddenly not so satisfying when the comic world is violated. Over time I've noticed that moment, I've seen the audience react at that moment when the world is breached.'

Turning to Samantha Baines, she has a gag in the *Telegraph*'s own list of best jokes from the Edinburgh Fringe 2017, where she adds a beforethought to a found payoff:

> I'm selling my old tennis equipment but I can't work out, what's the net worth?

This however wasn't her first brush with joke competitions as she had previously become the first woman in the final of the UK Pun Championships! (Yes, that is a real thing.) Samantha said to me:

> We were brought up with a tradition of men doing gags. Old-school comedians that we all love and quote, like Tommy Cooper. That was comedy for so long. People call them Dad jokes. I remember I was asked about that and I said, 'Mums like jokes too!' There's a school of thought that women tell each other stories and so are better at storytelling. Well, I do storytelling in my shows *and* I also love writing one-liners. I think there are a lot of female comedians out there doing it, like Adele Cliff, she's great, and Saskia Preston. Audiences can still be freaked out by a woman doing it but they are changing.

She went on:

> When I did the pun championship, we were given twenty subjects and we had to write one-hundred [gags] in two weeks. I was on my honeymoon looking up words! For my regular shows, I don't really look up words. Puns just come to me when I'm writing other things. I'll just be reading something and I'll see the double meaning. [For the competition] we had to write puns about dogs. I tried to write puns that haven't been written before, which is quite hard when you're looking at a subject like dogs. If you google dog puns, there are so many. I was trying really hard. Maybe I shouldn't have because it took me much longer! Then I started looking at the names of dogs that could be within other words, rather than just a double meaning. There was one that I did in the pun championship. I love it but the set-up is quite long, which is, 'I'm trying to convince my husband to get a dog.

I'm doing it subliminally through the wallpaper. I've bought this wallpaper with Irish Terriers on it. I'm not gonna lie, I've got an ul*terior* motive.'

It's hard to pick up on the page, but the pun is around ul*terior/terrier*. And yes, it does have a lengthy set-up, but I think Samantha gets away with it because there's a laugh in the first part of the set-up, when she says she's trying to convince her husband 'subliminally through the wallpaper.' That is amusing in itself because it's so absurd. I think if she gets a laugh there, it means she's got a bit of goodwill which buys her more time to complete the thought. Whereas if the set-up was that long but with nothing funny about it, it would be more of a stretch. 'I found it a really interesting and challenging writing process, to give myself a random subject and to have to write puns on it and I think I'll do that again.'

Before we met to speak together for this book, I wrote a joke for Samantha starting with a single ambiguous word and working backwards. Here, as an example, is a punning (meta) gag from Masai Graham:

I've written a joke about a fat badger, but I couldn't fit it into my set.[3]

This joke relies on the multiple meanings of the single word 'set'; it is one of the words with the most meanings in the English language. In this case it means both a badger's den and also the contents of a stand-up's performance (the word 'set' here being borrowed from the terminology used by musicians). To write a joke of this kind, I googled 'ambiguous words list' and here, semi-randomly, are words that apparently have nineteen meanings each (including 'set'): clear, draw, give, hold, set, bar, break, up, dry, dull, flash, level, live, part, pop, rule, separate, strip.

Straight away 'bar' leapt out at me. It's the basis of the old Tommy Cooper classic about walking into a bar and sustaining a head injury. Moving on, let's try and do something with 'pop'. My process in writing a gag based on this word was first of all to think of a context in which the word 'pop' might appear. The phrase 'pop the question' (as in propose) came to mind as Samantha had recently got married. I tried to write a gag using that phrase as a payoff, working backwards.

The next step was to try and take that phrase literally. How could you literally pop the question? Well, it must be inflated in some way. My first version had Samantha saying 'no' and her boyfriend then popping the balloon in a fit of pique, but as she actually said 'yes' I made it fit the facts – but that leaves the popping a little confusing as Samantha picked up on. Here is my first stab at the gag:

> My boyfriend got a helium-filled 'will you marry me?' balloon. And when I said 'yes' he stuck a pin in it. So, he popped the question.

When I presented this joke to Samantha, she said she could imagine herself using it, but that she would rewrite it to suit her: 'I thought I don't need the word "helium" because a balloon will be inflated anyway. And where you say a "will-you-marry-me" balloon, I'd just say he bought a balloon with "Will you marry me?" on it. "Stuck a pin in it" is also quite wordy, and why would he do that, so I thought it could accidentally burst.'

Samantha tends to add a more conversational dimension to her wordplay jokes: 'I will do a longer run-up to a pun, so people almost don't know it's going to be a pun. With the pop joke, I'd say "I recently got married!" and then they'd all go "Woo," and I'd go, "Thanks guys, do you want to know how he proposed?" And then I'd go into the joke':

> He's got a balloon with 'Will you marry me?' on it. He accidentally burst it. Yes, he popped the question.

Samantha went on: 'When the pun comes, it's not like, "Oh it's another one-liner," it's like "Oh, it's her life *and* it's a silly pun." Whereas your version: "My boyfriend got ...," that's more of one-liner comedian way to do things.' This process of re-writing the original comic idea exactly matches how stand-ups can take a gag or an idea suggested to them by a director (or a co-writer or another comic) and then, rather than saying it exactly as offered, rewrite it to make it their own.

The other thing that I find often happens is that the suggested joke or idea triggers off a new idea in the comic. And this is exactly what happened here: 'When you consider the word "pop," the first thing you think of is balloon, so what else would you think of that can pop that isn't a balloon? First, I just thought of other things that just have "pop" in it, like pop music or alcopop, then I thought of Pringles; "Once you pop, you just can't stop."' From this I wrote:

> My husband proposed by writing 'will you marry me' on a Pringles can. It's his third wedding. Once you pop, you just can't stop.

I was delighted to see this different take on the idea but wondered if an audience, hearing it cold, would make the connection with 'pop the question'. You'd need to set up the idea of popping the question but we couldn't see a way of doing that without giving away the key word 'pop'. It'd have to be something like this:

> It was such an exciting weekend when my husband popped the question. He proposed by writing 'will you marry me' on a Pringles can. It's his third wedding. Once you pop, you just can't stop.

This might work as it's 'popped' and not 'pop' in the set-up, but nevertheless as Samantha said, 'It feels like it just might be a little bit too tricky. A lot of the time I think I find that's the problem with puns. You're like, "It's a really good link but how can I make it work so that it makes sense, so that the set-up isn't so long winded?"'

In her festival shows, when Samantha writes about science subjects, the topics aren't especially common in comedy, so, I put it to her, 'There's a chance you might come upon a novel pun.' She replied: 'There's always a chance! Also, because my audiences are a bit savvy to my puns now, I've done things in my previous shows, like I had a "pun bell" in my first show, which I give to an audience member and they'd ring the bell [when they heard a pun]. They'll even laugh sometimes when I haven't intended it to be a pun.'

# 7

## It takes two:

## Incongruity, transpositions, analogies, personification and bathos

We began the book by discussing how two contrasting qualities in the stand-up's persona, archetypes or attitudes for instance, can come together to comic effect. In Chapter 2 we saw Bill Hicks bring together esoteric thinking and news reporting. And jokes tend to have two ideas that collide unexpectedly; for example, two meanings of a word, or a commonplace meaning of a phrase and an unexpected meaning.

Comedy is so often about two things unexpectedly coming together and creating a comic friction. In this chapter we will look more closely at three techniques that have come up already, *incongruity*, *transpositions* and *personification*, and we will introduce two more, *analogies* and *bathos*. All of these, in various ways, bring two things together. Having discussed these techniques in detail, we will explore them in action in Chapter 9 in stories and routines.

### Incongruity

For the last ten years, my old friend and colleague Barry Ferns has run a comedy show at the Edinburgh Fringe. So far so normal.

Except this show takes place on the top of Arthur's Seat, the dramatic extinct volcano that offers fantastic views over the city. It all began when he and I wrote and co-directed *This Sketch Show Belongs to Lionel Richie*, and we wanted to do eye-catching spin-off shows. One idea was *Dial-A-Sketch* where we published a number that people could ring to order a live performance of a sketch like a pizza. Another was the original Arthur's Seat show, which meant we had to register the mountain as a Fringe venue. To their credit, the Fringe Office allowed this. Barry has run this show every year since.

This whole event in itself creates *incongruity*. Taking all the familiar aspects of a comedy night and playing them out at the top of a windswept peak. Barry believes that 'you can make a club from anything if the intention is there and everybody wants to be there'. This was evidenced by the *Laughter in Odd Places* shows that included a gig in a launderette where audience members had to bring one item of clothing to wash, and more recently Maria Bamford in *Old Baby* performing stand-up in a front room, to people on a park bench, in a book shop and in a bowling alley. Incongruous settings all.

To make the windswept space at the top of Arthur's Seat work as a venue Barry observes that, 'Having a doorway really helps.' Barry sets up a door frame, and despite the 'club' being entirely open to the elements and accessible on all sides, people have to enter through the 'door'. He goes on, 'It's a funny idea and having a doorway and greeting people as they come in, means they then buy in to the idea of it being a comedy club a lot more.' They even stamp people's hands as they enter. Barry goes on, 'This incongruous environment makes it a lot more exciting for people. They feel they're part of something special. They tweet about it and post pictures on Instagram. They're having an experience rather than just watching a comedy show.'

*Incongruity*, while a term not necessarily in everyday use by working comics, certainly has a venerable philosophical history. In an academic paper, Oliver Double explains that 'the theory states that we laugh at a suddenly-perceived and unexpected clash of words, or mismatch of concepts, that we laugh when language or logic are used in an inhabitual manner; at its most basic level, we laugh at the incongruous'.[1]

He also discusses the superiority theory that states that laughter is generated when we feel better than the target of the joke. This rings true, and sometimes of course the target of the joke is the comic themselves. It is however easy to think of examples where this feeling would be produced without any merriment, whereas there does seem to be something inherently comic about incongruity. For completeness, the other main theory is 'release theory' which sees laughter as a release of tension, which certainly does happen in stand-up. For example, I saw Reginald D. Hunter relate the entire very dark plot of the short film *Bus 44*, building tension in the room that was released by a sudden gag at the end. Here the key thing with the set-up was that he played it totally straight and in deadly earnestness. When the release came, the laugh was huge because the tension had been so ratcheted up. You also see this in everyday life. If you see someone take a nasty fall and fear they may be seriously hurt, when they emerge unscathed there is laughter.

# Transpositions

While discussing the workings of comedy with Oliver Double we hit upon what seemed to be a helpful term. When I spoke with him, he began by telling me: 'It normally takes less than 30 minutes to get to work, it took well over an hour this morning. There was a ridiculous queue of traffic, and it all turned out to be due to one little set of temporary lights.' He went on to say, 'I don't know why I'm telling you this' but it turned out to be a good jumping-off point to explore *transpositions*.

If you were going to talk about this in stand-up, initially you'd tell it more or less as it was with a bit of exaggeration. And then you could imagine a set of those temporary lights in a Grand Prix, with all the racing drivers having to stop and queue up. (You could get this across through an act-out of the commentary perhaps.) I asked Oliver what terms he'd use to describe what's going on here:

> I would talk about 'bi-sociation' because your idea does fit Koestler's model. He wrote *The Act of Creation* which was the first bit of comic theory I ever read. Bi-sociation is 'bi' meaning two and the 'sociation' from association. It's associating two different things. There's always these two associative frames that clash in a given example and that's how he identifies the key conceptual device at the core of a joke [or comic idea]. You have two intersecting planes of discourse. In your example, the world

of ordinary driving [in his model] would be M1, and M2 would be competitive sports driving. And the L, the bit where they meet, is the fact they're both driving, and you've incongruously applied the logic of one situation to the other.

I explained to Oliver that I'd use the word 'juxtaposition' to describe what's going on here: normal driving and competitive driving have been juxtaposed. (Here comes the new term.) He responded, 'I think "juxtaposition" is fine as a word to describe that. You could also use *transposition* because you're transposing the logic of one onto the other.' I immediately felt this was a more powerful way of capturing this comic process, so much so that I now use the word *transposition* … as you can see. I asked Oliver if he used that term already and he responded: 'No, it just came out when we were talking. It just struck me that "juxtaposition" is about comparison, putting one thing next to another. Whereas "transposition," is taking something and putting it in a different context.'

And transposition is something comedy does a lot. A classic example is Eddie Izzard's *Death Star Canteen* where the very banal everyday realm of the 'canteen' is transposed into the very grand futuristic sci-fi realm of Star Wars. Izzard has Darth Vader queuing up for food and getting into a petty argument over trays. In terms of developing this idea, one approach would be to get a sheet of paper, put a line down the middle and in the left-hand column, put everything you can think of about canteens and in the right-hand column, everything you think of about *Star Wars*. Oliver discussed the piece:

> That's a perfect example. The worlds of science fiction and fantasy don't necessarily allow for much of the mundane features of reality, like the world of the boring institution, here summed up by the word 'canteen'. In Koestler's model, there is a logic that joins the two planes of discourse that are not commonly associated. Sometimes it's just the double meaning of a word, but here it's the not illogical train of thought that says, 'Well, if there's this number of people gathered, they must be being fed.' Of course, given that it's science fiction, you'd think they'd be given some kind of pack of protein gel or something but his solution is genius: There's a canteen. That's the incongruity he's working with. That's the first stage. And then, the second stage

is: What's the best way of expressing that so it's funny? Going from there to five minutes of top-quality stand-up, there's a lot in that: That's when he starts playing out the logic of the canteen on the Death Star with all the characterizations. That's when it starts to become funny.

Having set up the idea of a canteen on the Death Star, which gets a laugh just as a verbal concept, Izzard then acts out the premise. He shows us Darth Vader having a petty argument with a canteen worker and the reactions of an annoyed third person in the queue. It's an *act-out* (see Chapter 10). And it's very casually done, but the situation is vividly conjured up nonetheless.

# Bathos

The effect of Eddie Izzard's transposition, bringing a canteen into the Death Star, is to create *bathos*. Bathos is defined as a 'lapse in mood from the sublime to the ridiculous'. Once in class, I was talking about this kind of bathetic transposition (as I now call it), and someone in the group said: 'It's big/small', which is a succinct way of capturing what's going on. In the Death Star example, you've got the bigness of sci-fi and the smallness of this quibbling in a canteen, or in my original example the bigness of Formula One and the smallness of struggling to get into work.

This bathetic 'big/small' device is often used in satire. Typically, satire is comedy that is about something current, that is making a point and whose target is powerful. Oliver said to me, 'I remember becoming aware of how Mark Steel works with that often. He found an analogy for a political situation, in an everyday situation and then he'd act it out, using voices and so on. I had a conversation with him last week, and I told him that I'd noticed that quite early on, and he said, "Yes, that's how I'll do it." It's from the epic, and large, and grand, to the trivial and banal. It's funny to move between those levels.' This is a standard tactic of satire (see Jonathan Swift). Ahir Shah said to me:

There's something in the ludicrousness of the attempt [that can make it funny]. Towards the end of the show [*Control* 2017] I'm comparing the entire history of global inequality leading to fascism to *slightly going-off milk*. Just the brass neck of even offering to make the comparison I think will lend something to the humour. Also, I think when we're talking about macro issues, they tend to be too big for us even to comprehend. Any way in which you can humanize large issues is a way of making it more immediate to the audience's experience of the world.

You leave an Ahir Shah show in doubt of his opinions. He told me, 'Stand-up is the medium with which I put out the ideas that I want to talk about. If I'd gone down an academic route, I might have written books or given talks.' It's essential in creating satirical material to have a clear point you wish to make. You might observe, to take the current president, that 'Trump's got small hands' – but what point are you making? Oliver continued, 'The first time I heard Donald Trump's hands being joked about was by John Oliver and his point was excellent satire, which was to do with Trump's thin skin. It was the fact that he was upset about people joking about his hands, not to do with the hands themselves. That was what was funny. It was the hands as a way of understanding the psychology of the man; then you understand something more about the political situation.' He's taken a big issue and addressed it through something small. But then you can also go the other way, take something small and put it into something big which is what the Death Star canteen's doing, although in Eddie Izzard's case he's not really making a point. (Other than observing that a lot of mundanity is left out of these fantastical worlds.) Both of these transpositions are bathetic.

# Analogies

I commented to Oliver that *bathos* is found in literature too and he replied, 'A lot of things that happen in comedy can also be found in literature. For example, a lot of great comic lines, if done differently, would be a line in a poem because one of the basic units of creative endeavour is comparing one thing to another. Metaphor or simile in poetry or literature. That happens a lot in stand-up too, it's just that they wouldn't normally refer to it as a metaphor or simile. Bridget Christie has one where she says every individual's vagina is "like a snowflake made of gammon." The mind work that she's doing in creating that line is exactly the same as a poet would do, but it's just that in comedy you almost deliberately do it wrong. You do it so that the comparison jars rather than strikes you as beautiful. That's why you laugh I suppose.'

When we spoke, Tony Allen used the term *analogy* for this kind of comic effect, as does the founding editor of the *Onion*, Scott Dikkers, who defines it as 'comparing two disparate things'. Here is an example from the *Onion*: 'Man Approaches Unfamiliar Shower Knob Like He's Breaking Wild Stallion.'[2] I tend to use (for its punchiness) the phrasing 'is like'. This *is like* that. Ahir Shah observes, 'An analogy is being able to draw commonalities between different things and simultaneously make comments on both of them. When I analogize between Brexit and splitting up with my ex, I'm thinking "52 per cent of me is certain it has to happen."' People react: 'Oh, that *is* how relationships end. Because more than half of you feels this isn't the right thing to be doing.'

# Personification

'Personification' (or anthropomorphism) is when something non-human is given human characteristics and can speak. Mr Cee, who in chapter nine anthropomorphizes his tears, argues that 'everything's got a voice. The more we realize that the better.' I commented that Richard Pryor was the master of personification and Mr Cee agreed: 'A master. He gave animals voices. When you start doing that, you see the world from a different dimension.' For example, his sophisticated and picky pet dogs, when given their dog food, ask: 'Can we have some wine with that?' Ahir Shah gives a political example: 'In the last show [*Machines* 2016], when I was talking about climate change, I did a "dumb short play" [an act-out] of me pretending to be a tree having a conversation with a man about how our species produces energy.'

In a memorable routine, Noel Fielding acts out the everyday situation of having a bluebottle in the house that refuses to fly out of the open window. Described like this, it may not sound hugely promising as a subject for observational comedy. However, Fielding brings the routine brilliantly to life by taking the perspective of the bluebottle. He buzzes around the stage giving us a running commentary on how he is deliberately winding up the human.

Similarly, Jerry Seinfeld imagines what horses must be thinking when raced around a circular track. Following the 'big hurry' they find out to their bemusement that they're back where they started.[3] It's worth keeping this device in mind, and whenever you are doing a routine about an animal or an object ask yourself: What must it be thinking? Or what would it say? You don't even have to justify it suddenly talking since people are happy to suspend their disbelief and their minds are also well trained from childhood films and stories.

Most new comics don't use personification, and it can be a surprise and a delight for audiences when they have the confidence to do so. For example, on a recent course, one of the students was working on a fairly straightforward observational routine about being too drunk to get the key in the lock after a night out. This routine was lifted out of the commonplace and into something special when he personified both the key and the lock, and had them reacting like a man and a woman in an awkward, drunken sexual encounter.

In an example of what we might term *inner-personification*, Ed Byrne has terrified operatives in a man's brain desperately trying to think of the correct answer when the man's girlfriend asks him what he's thinking. The Numb Skulls from the *Beano* and the Pixar film *Inside Out* also offer good examples of this, and similarly, in one extraordinary Richard Pryor routine, he even gives a voice to his heart attack. Giving a voice to your inner states like fear, guilt or lust or even physical conditions means you can then be in dialogue with them rather than just talking about them.

# 8

# Developing and structuring stories and routines

I've had two recent sessions where turning true stories into stand-up was the common theme. The first was with a middle-aged man who was totally new to comedy and about to do his first open spot. For no particular reason, let's call him Gilbert. The second was with another middle-aged man but one who had been doing stand-up for years. Equally randomly, I am going to call him Slater.

Slater, while not yet fully pro, regularly does paid gigs. He'd reached a point however where he felt his stuff had stagnated. At the initial meeting with Gilbert, the would-be stand-up, he recited a series of anecdotes from his life (that go down a treat socially) with the expectation that I would laugh and say 'This is great stand-up material.' But the fact is it wasn't stand-up material. It's not that there was anything wrong with them as anecdotes but stand-up is not reciting funny stories. This took him aback. He thought all he had to do was go on stage and deliver these anecdotes well.

Slater on the other hand had been doing a successful act for years. He was, however, trotting out the same stuff over and over again and had been for a long time. This is not necessarily wrong, for while new comedians often think they have to keep coming up with new material you really don't have to. In fact, the people who are booking you would like to see you deliver the tried and tested stuff. Many club comedians for their own creative satisfaction or low boredom threshold do keep developing new stuff. There are, though, many who get by with the same material for years on end and Slater for a long time was one of those.

Slater's act was in large part based around self-deprecating one-liners where he made fun of his own appearance and failure with women. It was a cartoon version of himself, exaggerating his own failings to a grotesque degree. Now he wanted to bring in some truer stuff and draw on some real-life experiences. Slater knew that he had work to do to turn his true stories into stand-up which is why he had approached me. Gilbert had no idea he had any work to do but, after our first meeting, he suddenly discovered he had a lot of work to do.

# Turning true stories into stand-up

What is this work? First, I often say to acts: stand-up is not a documentary or a witness statement. You can exaggerate, edit and lie. For example, if someone said something embarrassing maybe you could change *who* said it. Perhaps instead of a random person it could be your mother who said it. It's based on something that's real, but you're going to be changing elements of it to try and get more out of it. Mr Cee responded:

> For me, that's so important. You're not a news reporter you're a comedian. For example, you might have a story where you're in the bedroom with your very first girlfriend. You've got your pants down. She's got her pants down. And her mum comes through the door. Now you could tell that story to your family and friends and they'll laugh for half-an-hour. A stand-up audience aren't going to laugh anything like that. So, [as director] you say to the person, 'If it wasn't the mum, who came in?' Some people will say, 'Oh, her dad.' I'd say 'Forget the dad. Who else?' They'd go: 'The grandma!' Now we're getting somewhere. 'Okay, so what does the grandma say?' Then they come back with: 'What are you doing to my granddaughter?!' No. Grandmother doesn't say that. She says: 'Oh *hello* young man.'

As well as changing people and places in the true stories, you can also up the ante. This is where you exaggerate (or totally fabricate) the seriousness or significance of the situation, or the pressure you were under. If there is nothing at stake and you are under no pressure the funniness is reduced – or even absent. You can increase the funniness of any kind of situation by:

- Increasing the time pressure. Give the situation a deadline or exaggerate its imminence. If in real life this piece of work you messed up didn't have to be in for two weeks, instead make out it had to be in the next day.

- Introducing a witness. Your awkwardness or embarrassment or struggle will always be worse (and so funnier) if it's happening in front of someone. Their reactions will be a key part of the comedy.

- Making the context more significant. For example, if the story was about you saying something stupid down at the pub with your mates, how about changing it to being in a posh restaurant on a date?

- Decreasing your own skills or efficacy in the situation; play it dumb. As Logan Murray said to me: 'Stand-up is not so much about the story. It's more about the idiot in the story.'

On that last point, in my coaching, I often show a clip of US comic Brian Regan, an *innocent jester,* telling a story of how he was confused and intimidated when he called parcel service UPS to pick up some boxes.[1] It is a great example of a comic playing it dumb. Apparently based on a real situation, the crux of the joke is that the authoritative voice on the end of the phone wants to know the 'girth' of the boxes and Regan has no idea what 'girth' means; but he will not admit to this and attempts to bluff his way through it. He also doesn't have suitable scales to weigh the parcel. It's in his increasingly desperate attempts to get them to pick up his boxes that the comedy lies.

Regan *exaggerates* both how brusque the UPS guy is and also how stupid he himself is. In his story Regan moves between narrating the action and then actually portraying it. There is strong physicality in the performance and it is filled with act-outs (see Chapter 10). He doesn't confine himself to acting out what literally happened. He also acts out what *might have happened.* For example, having discovered that he can't see the numbers if he puts the parcel on the bathroom scales to weigh it, he pounces and whips the box away to try and reveal the weight before it returns to zero. He tries many ways to solve this problem without acknowledging there is a problem.

# Structuring a story or routine

Stand-up is so often about things that are wrong, absurd or not working in some way. Coming up with absurd, unexpected or counter-intuitive solutions ('What would solve it?') can be a funny place to take a rant or a story. And, as in the Brian Regan example, attempting to deal with a problem but lacking the skills or insight to do so is a cornerstone of comic action. I have developed this model to describe how a piece of comic writing can unfold:

**Set-up:** prepares the ground, gives the audience all the information they need.
**Reveal:** reveals the clear, central comic idea.
**Escalation:** the idea is pushed so that it becomes more and more absurd.
**Payoff:** a comic twist.
(It can be seen how this relates to Set-Up/Payoff/Topper(s)/ Tag.)

In terms of my structure, the Brian Regan story unfolds like this:

**Set-up:** we moved, I had boxes to get taken away, I called UPS, you need info to hand when you ring them.
**Reveal:** I am clueless about the technicalities.
**Escalation:** the various attempts to get round this limitation.
**Payoff:** I lie to get the job done.

So, he sets up the situation, the given circumstances: crucially, just giving the facts and *not* saying anything about his inadequacies in the situation. When people are telling a story socially they tend to vocalize the main thing straight away. Mr Cee observes, 'If the audience doesn't see it coming, it'll have a bigger impact when it lands. For example, I would never use the line, [which he says ruefully] "Oh my! You're never gonna believe what happened with me and this girl I saw last night." Then when I tell you it was something negative, there's no surprise because of how I've set it up. Whereas, if I say: "Oh my God. This girl I saw last night. She was beautiful!" Now you're expecting some big, wonderful story. Because of my energy here, I've misdirected you. When the negative hits, you've already bought into the positive energy so it's going to surprise you.'

In the same way, Brian Regan doesn't start by saying 'You won't believe how stupid I was when I phoned up to get some boxes picked up!' He just sets it up straight, and *then* reveals the comic idea. In improvisation terms, this is the 'game' of the piece: He is trying to get a package picked up without the required skills and knowledge. This piece is then focused on this one clear comic idea, escalating it to greater and greater levels of absurdity until it's capped off with a comic finish.

A related problem in terms of beginning a set can stem from the advice that is often given to new comedians: to *start with their funniest joke*. The logic of this is, of course (if it works), that you start with a big laugh which relaxes you and the audience; they now trust that you are funny. On one level this makes sense, but I have worked with several acts whose opening was distorted by this apparent need to start with a really strong gag. It led them to coming out with something quite extreme or bizarre. Yes, they got a laugh, but it made for a forced, unnatural start and was difficult to continue from it. It also left them nowhere to build to. Instead, it can be better to start more naturally.

When you look over a routine ask yourself: Where does this begin? *I always suggest finding a natural jumping-off point.* A good example came up recently when I worked with a stand-up who had material about ageing. He would just launch into it at the start of his set, with no reason or context. We reworked it so that, since he was the right age for this to work, he started by saying something like: 'I looked in the mirror this morning and discovered my first grey hair.' Now there is a personal and compelling reason for him to be thinking about ageing, and so the audience can readily connect with him and engage with his thoughts on the topic.

There are many ways of getting into the topic, and a good rule of thumb is to make it current and personal. This approach helps the audience forget that the whole thing is a massive contrivance to make them laugh. It makes it feel more like a natural social interaction. In my directing, I regularly take comics through this approach, finding the personal, chatty, current, natural jumping-off points for material. This really freshens it up and wins the audience over. It's a seemingly small change, but it makes a big difference.

Here's the outline of an example routine from new comic Neil Ackroyd. I worked with him one-to-one and he took me through some material. Standing on stage in front of me in a room above a pub in Soho, the material unfolded like this:

- He began by introducing a complex system (named with an acronym) of judging the effort put in versus the kudos gained of any given activity. If you don't entirely follow that, then you are in the position of me (his audience at that point) who didn't really follow it either. This was a lot of complex information to digest and make sense of, plus there was no context for it.

- He then went on to explain that he was lazy and vain. Now the audience will be less sure they like this person. He didn't give an example of his laziness and vanity; he just said it. It was a case of *telling* not *showing*. There also wasn't a joke attached to this fact. It was just information. So, he has started this short routine by overloading the audience with confusing detail and then making himself potentially dislikeable.

- Then he said he'd recently done something that required practically no effort on his part but that people were impressed by. What could this be? Then he revealed it was a charity skydive. Things picked up at this moment. Maybe we like him after all thought the imaginary audience. Then he said he was strapped to someone else who did all the difficult stuff and he could just be lazy. Now it's starting to become potentially funny.

- He went on to say that for very little effort he got an enormous amount of kudos, so it scored well on the system he introduced at the start. Ah ha! Now we understand what he was on about. The audience might now be with him, but it's been a slog. Or they may have switched off some time ago.

There is nothing inherently wrong with the potential funniness of this idea or indeed with the likeability of the person delivering the material. What is wrong is structural. Where would you choose instead to begin this routine? For me there is only one place to start this routine. The best and most effective starting point is: You reveal you did a charity skydive. Why? The audience will engage with this as it's a personal story. They will also start warming to you and wanting to hear more. I suggested that the routine would best unfold like this:

- Reveal you did a charity skydive.
- Explain that it required practically no effort on your part (you were strapped to someone else who did all the difficult stuff).
- And yet for very little effort you say you got an enormous amount of kudos.
- Introduce a complex system (named with an acronym) of judging the effort put in versus the kudos gained from any given activity. *And score the skydive on this scale.*
- You wondered what other activities would score well.

This is the best way to work through this material and it was funnier when done like this. The audience will be engaged by the idea of the charity skydive; especially if it's presented as a recent event. Even when it was a long time ago, the best start would be, 'Last weekend I did a skydive.' The immediacy gives it life but also it seems less like a contrived routine and more like a genuine desire to share something that has just happened. Furthermore, everyone gets the idea of a charity skydive so there is nothing new or complicated to understand.

This is the set-up (and potentially simple laughs could be found while setting it up). Then the reveal of the joke is that very little effort was required. The idea is then escalated with the observation that for not much effort *a lot* of kudos was received. The payoff is the system that has been devised to measure this. It can then branch out into a related routine that asks: what other activities would score well? Alternatively, later on in the set, he could introduce another unconnected activity and then, as a callback, unexpectedly score it using the system. And note the one that I dropped: You explain you are lazy and vain. In the new version, we infer this – it's shown not told.

Neil has adopted this way of thinking: 'Now I write the boring waffle version knowing that later I will think "Where would Chris start it?" Then I rewrite the routine starting there. Before I just kept trying to write the perfect intro and got stressed and wasted time.'[2] And this is the best way to use this structure. Write a whole lot of stuff as an overly long first draft and *then* work with what you have to edit, punch it up with gags and put it into an effective structure.

# 9

# Set-up/payoff in stories
# and routines

Having looked at the writing and rewriting of one-liners as more-or-less standalone entities in Chapters 5 and 6, let's now look at jokes in the contexts of stories and routines. Whether they are verbal, visual or act-outs, you need to find the set-up/payoffs *within* the story as you work towards the climactic payoff. In Chapter 5 we discussed how the words of others can be *found set-ups* for jokes, but they can also be *your own words*. This is where you may have innocently spoken or written a phrase without intending any comic possibilities, but then when you return to it you suddenly see a potential joke. In this way, sometimes the comedian *themselves* unwittingly produces a set-up.

## Voices A and B

Try producing a long rough version of your story, rant or discussion by speaking into a voice recorder. Don't worry about how funny it is, you're just getting something to work with. Leave it for a while, maybe a day or two, and then come back to it, treating the recording like Voice A, but you are now in the mindset of Voice B. So now you need to jump in with undermining, satirizing and cheeky comments, and try to do this as often as possible. You can then keep the cream of these comments, editing the original story to take out the non-funny comments that didn't take you anywhere. You then inhabit both of these voices on stage – Voice A is the set-up and Voice B is the payoff.

This idea of a Voice A being on a particular path, and then your Voice B diverting it, is explored in an exercise where I get five people to work together, like a multi-headed comedian, to build a 'routine'. The group of five comes to the front, lines up and a sixth person sits in front of them. This sixth person is the 'pointer', and it is their job to determine who of the five is speaking at any given moment. When someone is being pointed at, they speak. As soon as the pointer switches to someone else the original speaker has to stop and the new person picks it up and continues the routine as if one person is speaking. The charm of it comes from the unexpected turns the routine takes.

These twists tend to come as it switches from one person to another. The original speaker (Voice A), let's say, is on one train of thought. Then, when it switches to the next person (Voice B), they take it off on a tangent that we, the audience (not to mention the previous speaker), weren't expecting. Recall that here it is set up as one person speaking. This kind of thing happens: [Voice A] I was in such a hurry to get out of the house, that I pulled on my shirt and jacket and rushed out the door; [Voice B] then I realized I wasn't wearing any trousers. This exercise replicates the kind of in-the-flow gag that could come up socially.

Logan Murray uses a lot of improvisation in his stand-up training: 'Improv is a very good way of hot-housing idiot opinions. The idiot who exists between those two heads is a very creative, funny person.' Sometimes, as with found set-up jokes, these interactions can be converted to stand-up. In the game, we're imagining it's one person speaking, but in stand-up these kinds of switches in perspective really are produced by the one person who is speaking. In your stand-up set you are in effect both Voice A and Voice B: 'I was in such a hurry to get out of the house, that I pulled on my shirt and jacket and rushed out the door. Then I realised I wasn't wearing any trousers.'

The main point of these games however is not to yield material but to get new comics thinking in a particular way. Logan Murray: 'I do the improvs on the course to make people realize they're funny, they're born funny, and to get them used to reacting to somebody else's ideas. You simply react [to the other person] and say the asshole thing. Once people get a feeling for going into that territory, it's a small step to starting to react to your own stuff. They can just chuck their brains out and some stupid remark may come up that will make the audience laugh.'

Afterthoughts don't just lead to one-liners. This kind of thinking can be used to gag up a routine or an entire show. When Logan Murray directs a show, he is often in this frame of mind, looking for the afterthoughts. He told me:

> I tend to just fuck around and the bits that make us laugh go into the next draft. You could say basically I'm a one-trick pony when it comes to a creativity! If you let me off the lead I tend to over-gag everything. Then on the second draft you turn your editor back on. This week a really good comic came round; won awards, very good. At the moment, they have something which is, by their own admission, more like a TED talk. It's still really entertaining and detailed, that's the important thing. They've done the hard work. Then I'm the dick in the corner adding stupid afterthoughts. That's an easy job to do. Arguably, the hardest job is to actually come up with the idea. Then I'll just say the stupid thing undercutting the thoughts they've created.

On my stand-up course, a new comic had had the experience of walking along the canal and seeing a man with a plastic bag of dog poo – but no dog. In fact, the dog soon appeared from some bushes, but before that she had wondered what on earth the man was up to. It struck her that this might make a short piece but she didn't know how to turn it from an observation of something (briefly) incongruous into stand-up.

Let's begin at the beginning. First of all, we need to set up the basic information. Sometimes the set-up is not funny in itself, just short and factual like the Brian Regan UPS routine we discussed in Chapter 8. But here I wanted to try and get some laughs in the set-up. (A set-up can be funny. You just haven't yet revealed the central comic idea.) For example, when she was working out the set-up it started: 'It was a lovely day and I had nothing to do so I decided to walk along the canal.' I felt there could even be a possible laugh from this opening line. After a bit of brainstorming we reorganized it into the set-up/payoff structure, adding a beforethought:

> I had loads of work to do, the house was a mess, deadlines to meet. So, I decided to go for a walk along the canal.

This got a laugh of recognition from the group. We have now found a first laugh *in the set-up*. Note that the story is starting to be fictionalized to find extra laughs. Here it's better if the speaker is really busy that day – upping the ante. It's also Voice A and B writing. Voice A is aware of her responsibilities and deadlines, but Voice B doesn't care and wants to avoid it and prevaricate. This particular student was into meditation and as she developed the set-up she said: 'I was totally present, neither lost in the past nor planning for the future, absolutely in the moment. And I saw a man walking towards me' It's clearly Voice A saying this stuff about being mindfully present. It's crying out for the piss-taking Voice B to jump in and undermine it:

> I was totally present, neither lost in the past nor planning for the future, absolutely in the moment. Then I fell in the canal … . I didn't! I carried sure-footedly on my way.

Notice that Voice A comes back in after Voice B to keep it on track. Here we see that Voice B can jump in with any undermining, mocking statement to produce a potential laugh and then Voice A can return us to the flow of the story. Now we are ready for the *reveal*.

> And I saw this man walking towards me. He had a little plastic bag of poo. And no dog.

Here is the rule of three with a clear payoff, so even though it's a story, we are still using joke rhythms. Now the comic idea has been revealed, the escalation is pure speculation. The first question to ask, which you can voice in the piece is:

> Why on earth was he carrying a bag of poo without a dog? Was he taking it home to feed to his pet fly?

And there's a payoff from answering the question. Some more speculation can be done. Perhaps with some act-outs of her looking at him; he perhaps behaving shiftily and she becoming more suspicious. Is this for some perverse sexual practice? But then the dog appears and everything is back to normal. You now need a payoff. To generate one, you could treat the dog's appearance as a *false dawn*. By which I mean for a moment it seems like the absurdity is resolved – but then suddenly it isn't. For example, having had your mind put at rest, the actual owner of the dog could also emerge from the bush sending her mind reeling once more.

# Set-up/payoff in a story

When we met, Mr Cee talked about building bridges from the truth to comic ideas. He gave as an example a gag from his own set. The original joke was:

> A lot of people say to me, 'Cee, how did you get into comedy?' I say, 'It was simple. It was a life-changing decision. My employer sacked me.'

This is true and expressed in a simple set-up/payoff joke. First of all, note that he has worked forwards here. Someone (genuinely) asked him how he got into comedy and as a conversational joke he arrived at the payoff: 'My employer sacked me.' That was the starting point. He goes on, 'From that, I thought, "What actually happened?"' Note that a question kicks off the creative process. The answer? 'I had a disciplinary meeting and the truth is I wanted to work my notice but they said, "No just go straight away. Clear your desk."' This now is working backwards, he's going back in time from the moment of the original joke. Mr Cee explains to the audience about having to clear his desk and then says:

> And they gave me a box to put all of the stuff in. I thought, 'Wow. You know, for seven years of hard work, this is all I get? An empty box?'

Then he brings in how he felt:

> It was a tearful moment for me but I wasn't going to cry in front of everybody. Because I'm from the streets of North West London. Bad men don't cry. I kept saying to myself: 'Don't cry Cee, don't cry. Bad men don't cry.' Then my tears fall and they go 'Bad men don't wear glasses either.'

The speaking tears are an example of *personification*. Mr Cee observed, 'From that one question, "How did you get into stand-up?" I've built bridges that take me there to being sacked, to leaving the office, getting into a cab, going to my mum's house.' From there he goes into an act-out with his mum saying:

> 'What do you want to do with your life? What is your passion? What is your dream?' I said, 'Mum, I've always loved comedy and I've always wanted to teach.' She said, 'Teaching's a good job.' 'Yes, and I'm going to do comedy.' 'As I said, teaching is a good job.'

Then her punchline is:

> No matter what happens, remember this one thing…. You cannot come back and live here.

And this is *misdirection*. We expect the mother to say something like: 'I will always love you' – but she doesn't. So even though it's a *story* and not a sequence of one-liners, it's still operating as set-up/payoff with misdirection. When people say storytelling comics 'don't do jokes' they miss the fact that while, yes, they might not be doing wordplay, they *are* often still employing the same fundamental techniques.

Let's now look at some material from Josie Long, a *caregiver crusader*, which I quote with her permission. This is a true story from the start of her *Trying is Good* show.[1] She talks about going to the swimming pool in Edinburgh, looking down from the gallery over the pool and seeing that there is a kids' floating obstacle course in the water. This example is a conversational routine and the language is loose and natural with a tight structure, clear progression and a sequence of gags.

There is also a great deal in the performance that makes this funny that can only be hinted at on the page. This is a three-minute routine. It's striking when listening closely to the routine to notice that it's got a kind of natural, conversational untidiness as if she is finding the exact wording in the moment. I have indicated where the audience laugh as, for all its naturalness, Josie is working up to these moments and timing and delivering them precisely. At the outset, she explains that she originally wrote the show for the Edinburgh Fringe, and then goes on:

> The day I got to Edinburgh I decided to join a gym. Because this kind of figure doesn't maintain itself, I'll tell you that for free.

[laughter] Again your laughter is just like a knife, that's what it's like. [laughter] I was waiting in the leisure centre to fill out the membership card and I was in their office, which was in a gallery that looked down over the swimming pool. So, while I was waiting I was looking down at all the children in the pool – not in a paedophile way, [laughter] just in a normal adult way. And I noticed that what they'd got, what they constructed, was a kids' play scheme. And what it was, was a sort of floating obstacle course going from one side of the pool to the other, made up of all these interconnected inflatable rafts. And on each one was a little thing like a palm tree or a crab or a slide. And there were lots of very little children, very tentatively trying to navigate their way across it. Then at the side of the pool there was a man ... whose job it was ... was to stand there *with a powerful hose!* [laughter] Just picking them off. Getting rid of the weak. [laughter] Which is one thing, until you realize that's his job! Like at dinner parties people can go, 'Oh sorry Euan, what do you do for a living?' [posh Edinburgh accent, self-satisfied attitude] 'Oh me? I hose children off a floating assault course. That's what I do. [laughter] How long have I been doing it? Twenty-five years, I'm the best in the business.' [laughter] 'Why do you do that?' 'Presumably to upset them, I don't know. I don't enjoy my work.' But the thing is, he was really enjoying it. And he was focussing pretty much all his energy on one boy. And the boy he'd chosen was a properly tubby, like a properly obese boy. And what he was trying to do was get on and stay on an inflatable slide. And he had this absolute look of abject terror on his face. [scattered sympathetic laughter] Like at that minute he'd been let down by the entire adult world and he'd never forget. It was now just a countdown until he got a big gun collection, that's all it was. [laughter] And I was really feeling for him because I was an obese child and if I'm honest I'm still in the ballpark at the moment... . He looked like at that minute he'd realized something about life and what he'd realized was: Whenever you have something nice in this life, like a nice inflatable slide, there'll always be some prick – in a polo shirt – wanting to sluice you off of it. [laughter]

This is a good example of how a true story can be structured as a series of set-ups and payoffs to turn it into a stand-up routine; which, unlike a pub anecdote, demands frequent laughs. If you strip out these payoffs, you would find a gag-free version of this opening that would be perfectly serviceable in terms of relating the situation. When Josie Long refers to the ostensible pain caused to her by the audience's laughter, this is *metacomedy*. It is self-referential, comedy about the process of doing comedy. Overall, we can see that the structure of the routine is: set-up – joined a gym in Edinburgh, saw the obstacle course. Reveal – there was a man hosing the kids off of it. Notice how it's carefully constructed to build to the *reveal* of the man with the powerful hose. Also, we might speculate that some of the children were quite boisterous, but it makes for a funnier image that they are all 'tentative' and then more of a dramatic switch when we get to the hose reveal.

Then the *escalation*: *That's* his job … . She imagines that at dinner parties people ask him: 'Euan, what do you do for a living?' And she has him reply in a posh Edinburgh accent that he's been doing it for 25 years and that he's the best in the business. This creates incongruity, transposing the swimming pool job into a context where we would expect people to be talking about professions, the kinds of jobs where you could be recognized as 'best in the business' and could have a twenty-five-year career. In Josie Long's story, there is plenty of authentic detail and she maintains the realist authenticity with exaggeration that is minor. For example, she may well have exaggerated how terrified (or how overweight) the boy was or how much the man was focusing on him and enjoying it. We recognize the dynamic she describes and the victim/aggressor roles even if it is playing out in an incongruous context; the bullying of the fat boy by an authority figure is played out in an inherently absurd situation.

Crucially when she goes into the incongruous with the dinner party act-out this is clearly flagged as not being true – it's speculation. This is an important distinction and a very useful distinction to be clear about in a routine. I have often worked with comics who don't make this leap into *speculation*. It's here that the biggest laughs of this routine are found. And I have also worked with comics who do take their routine or story into an absurd realm but keep on presenting it as truth. This then hits the block of the audience thinking: That didn't happen. It's not that the idea wouldn't be funny, but it would be less funny. The audience laughter would be inhibited by them questioning the veracity of the story. All of this is resolved by making it clear it's speculative.

At the start of his first stand-up DVD *Cosmic Jam*,[2] Bill Bailey asks: Who photographs kebabs? This query could well have been born one night in a fast food outlet, seeing the photographs of the dishes on the menu and suddenly wondering who took them. If you've wondered about this yourself the pleasure is in hearing this thought being given voice. If not, it invites you to suddenly see the absurdity of something you'd not really thought about. It resembles the Josie Long piece in that he too has identified an absurd job and he also goes on to speculate about the person who does the job. He asks if he had illusions of being a great fashion photographer or a war correspondent, but he couldn't get the work and ended up on 'the old snack food circuit'. Notice the bathos here where the grandiosity of his dreams is being built up only to be knocked down. Bailey then goes on to imagine our photographer being asked socially about his work. This time though, rather than the dinner party setting of the Josie Long piece, he puts the photographer 'down the pub'. This feels absolutely the right location for this to play out. It's about his fall from grace rather than elevating him.

Initially he is cagey but after a few pints he is holding forth on all the takeaway foods he has photographed. Bailey develops the idea with an act-out where the photographer is in an attic, with a kebab on a cushion and photographing it in the manner of a soft-porn photographer. It is certainly *incongruous* to see food being photographed in that way. It transposes soft-porn photography into the world of food photography. So, stories and observations from life that have a spark of comedy are only the beginning. As we have seen across the last two chapters, there is an extensive process to get from there to an effective piece of stand-up. And yet, at the end of it all it should appear like the comic has just wandered up and started chatting. The art is to conceal the art.

# 10

# Directing the stand-up performance

Audiences don't laugh at writing. They laugh at a *performance* and if you can deliver a brilliant one you can make mediocre writing really sing. But if you're doomed to deliver a weak performance it will kill even brilliant writing. Let's conclude this section by discussing the directing of the performance. And given the centrality of this performance, the director often applies a lighter touch than you might expect.

Directing stand-up tends to be very different from directing actors. Actors often receive specific instructions on every nuance of a performance, which they are expected to replicate night after night. That kind of individual attention tends not to work for stand-up direction. Oliver Double commented: 'You simply can't do it like it's a play. Comedians have to feel that, while they're performing, they're in charge: This is *them* having an encounter with that audience right here, right now. They can't be thinking, "I need to pull my face into this shape right now," or "It's best to take a breath at this point." I think as a comedian you don't even think about it. You just do it, and it might change anyway from night to night.' And Samantha Baines told me:

> When I worked [on her 2016 show] with a director, she mostly supported me and helped me edit the script, rather than directed the performance. Sometimes she would give line readings: 'Say it like this.' And once, she said, 'I think you're losing the laugh, because you're going up at the end of the sentence and they expect something more, go down.' Then I did it and it got a

bigger laugh. … I wouldn't have been able to cope if I didn't have her. She kept me going. When you're trying it out and you mess a bit up, and you can't get it back to the way it used to be funny, my director was definitely picking me up and going, 'Go back out and do it again' or 'Maybe rethink it this way.'

I find directing a stand-up performance is about letting it run where it's working and zooming in at moments that require it. One thing I often find myself doing is exploring different ways of delivering a line. Here as an example, courtesy again of Dave's Funniest Joke of the Fringe award, is a Dan Antopolski gag:

I've been reading the news about there being a civil war in Madagascar. Well, I've seen it six times, and there isn't.

How might you deliver this? There are two main options. One is to say it *as a joke*; you are aware of the deliberate confusion of Madagascar the country and *Madagascar* the film. You, the joke teller, are in on the joke and are pointing out the ambiguity. A richer way to deliver the joke would be to speak it from a place of ignorance; you are not aware of the mistake you're making. What's more, you are annoyed by the stupidity of the news and are asserting your authority (you've seen it six times for crying out loud!) To you this is not even a joke, it's a simple statement of fact. Here the audience knows what's going on, but you don't: *dramatic irony*. And of course, the audience recognizes that the writer/performer behind the joke knows what the game is but is willing to suspend their disbelief. Kate Smurthwaite gets comics she is directing to work on their delivery of individual lines with her:

I get them to stand up and say it in 10 different ways. I believe most of us spend 80 per cent of our time writing lines and only 20 per cent thinking about how to say them. And what audiences enjoy is 20 per cent the lines and 80 per cent how they are said! Even if the opening line is, 'Hello I'm from Newcastle,' actually that's much funnier in a French accent. There's always something you can do with your voice or physicality that makes the line funnier. The difference between saying, 'I do a lot of speed dating,' in a normal way, and saying, 'I do a lot of speed dating,' and then slightly scratching your groin is one isn't a joke and one is a huge joke. So, I do that a lot, getting people to do the line over and over again: What can we do with this line, how can we get it funny?

To zoom in even closer, it can be effective to look for a change in attitude from the set-up to the payoff. To illustrate this, here's another Dave joke from Mark Watson:

I've been happily married for four years – out of a total of ten.

In your delivery of this joke, attitude wise, you might try:

[Positive, light] I've been happily married for four years [ruefully] out of a total of 10.

The switch in attitude could help the gag get more of a laugh. Certainly, if you were already rueful in the set-up it'd jar with what you're saying and would telegraph the payoff. Here is a Dave's Funniest Joke of the Fringe award gag from an actual Dave (Dave Green) with attitudes suggested for the set-up and payoff:

[Engaged, pondering] If I could take just one thing to a desert island...
[dismissive] I probably wouldn't go.

# Timing

One factor that everyone knows is important in comedy performance is 'timing'. Timing though is often felt to be a magical or mysterious thing that some people possess and others don't. And yet, like any skill that is deployed in a comedy performance, it can be learnt and it can be improved. Timing is: knowing when to pause ... and for how long. So, where are these pauses? There might be a slight pause (a beat) between a set-up and a payoff that old-school comics refer to as 'teeing up the joke'. To put it more generally, there are pauses of anticipation where some expectation or tension has been built up and then the comic waits...
...before providing the release. And there will overwhelmingly be a pause after the gag has landed to allow the audience to respond – with laughter, a groan, silence, pity, whatever. There will be some

people who are naturally better at this than others but all comedians can improve their timing and the outside eye of a director coaching the performance can help here.

I'm working at the moment with a relatively new act who has been invited to do a ten-minute set at the Montreal Comedy Festival. I am working on angling her material for North America and I am coaching her with her timing. Watching videos of recent sets she has performed in the UK, I got the strong impression she'd gone on stage with too much material and was rushing through it in order to fit it into the time allowed. When this happens, any idea of timing has been sacrificed. You don't have the time or the space to inhabit, enjoy and play with the spaces between things.

This is not uncommon among newer acts. I discussed this tendency with Oliver Double and he observed, 'That's a misunderstanding of the basic nature of the job. The job is not to get through the material. The basic nature of the job is to be funny for a given length of time.' Naturally, the first thing to do to address this issue is to go on with less material than you need. With a chatty delivery and audience laughter it'll probably fill the time and if not, no one will care if you go off early.

Many newer acts struggle to get the pace right. Geoff Whiting observed that at the start timing is not on many new acts' minds:

> They don't actually think about the timing when they perform it at first, they just think about the joke. A lot of new comics will come to me after the gig, and ask why didn't that joke work? And often I'll say, 'You didn't time it correctly. There is nothing wrong with it. If you deliver it differently you'll get a good laugh.' I've seen acts that have been going fifteen years, and on certain jokes they still get the timing wrong. These are very experienced people who are generally funny, but one gag doesn't work. And I think, I can't believe they can't see it; if they just change the speed of that gag, it will work.

Geoff advised Richard Lindesay on his pace when he was a new act: 'When he started, he used to deliver lines a bit too fast. Every comic who's nervous goes too fast. Even after years of experience, if they get a difficult corporate audience for instance, they go too fast. I said to Richard "You're good, you can slow down and leave pauses, and people aren't going to heckle or anything." He's doing it now, and it's working really well.'

This is the introduction of timing and the first step is just slow down. That's not to say that there is a uniform pace for all comics, some are faster than others. But whether you are naturally high paced or low, it's about the material unspooling at such a rate where you can be in control of the rhythm.

Geoff went on, 'Early on, Richard's timing wasn't quite right. If you watch one-liner acts, the timing – which Milton Jones has got spot on – is a big part of it. Sometimes Richard didn't leave enough of a pause in the right place when he was doing a one-liner. I just advised him to leave a gap in the sentence: Now he's doing it, and it's working.'

Richard sees his development in delivering his material as 'a move from saying material to explaining it'. He told me, 'I've got a background in IT where you have to explain complicated concepts to people who are not familiar with them. There's a parallel there, where I'm thinking "What information do the audience need, how much should I feed them at a time for them to assimilate it, and in what order should I give it to them?"'

As well as working with stand-ups, Geoff is an act himself. Unlike Richard Lindesay's one-liner style, Geoff's act is chatty and has the feel of storytelling. And as we have seen, even a chatty comedian is still essentially doing jokes. Geoff described to me how the pausing, the timing and emphasis very much still applies: 'Storytelling, just as much as one-liners, has got to be paced and timed. I do a true story about being on a plane before take-off.' Geoff is a nervous flyer and on this occasion, he is demanding to get off. The pilot comes out and talks to Geoff to calm his nerves and the pilot says, '"Take my advice, sit back and have a couple of large glasses of white wine … *I* have."' Geoff went on, 'There has to be that pause. If you don't leave the gap before, "*I* have," that kills it. Even though it's a storytelling gag not a one-liner, it's the same principle.'

Geoff finds there comes a point where this kind of timing is happening mostly automatically: 'It takes a lot of stage time to get really good timing. In my case I'd say about three or four years in, I'd nailed the timing. I think some people may have more of an innate ability with timing. But with some comics it has to be drummed into them. You have to really coach them to get it right.'

Oliver Double explained how he coaches timing with his university stand-up students: 'I show them specific clips where I'm looking at the use of pauses. There's a clip of Stephen Carlin and one of Susan Calman, and I watch it with them and point out: They pause there because the next line is a really funny line and they don't want you to just rush past it, they want you to feel the value of it. But you can't impose a method on them, even about pauses, it has to be their own rhythm. I also show them Mark Watson who doesn't really pause at all.'

Some students were able to apply that general instruction to their work. 'What I found was, when I assessed the performance, I noticed there were acts where I'd say, "You got that [laugh] because you put a pause in. That's what made that line work." So, you look at the fine grain so that they think about what they're doing in detail, gain a learned sense of how performance works and then internalize it.' So, at first, they consciously do it. Then in the end the direction is forgotten and they just do it.

I discussed timing with the Montreal-bound act, and gave her some example line readings (but of course the act needs to make the rhythm and timing her own). I may take a leaf out of Oliver Double's book and set her some clips to watch. In the meantime, I set an exercise I always give to stand-ups who need to work on their delivery: Arrange to meet with a friend in a bar or busy café. Sit opposite them and deliver your act in such a way that anyone passing by will think it's just conversation. Your friend needs to support you in this by nodding and giving small conversational responses. This engenders a natural delivery that is paced conversationally and it also begins to sort out the timing as you are pacing it around your friend's comprehension and reactions.

## TED talks

If you'll permit me a tangent at this point, I'd like to side-step to the world of TED talks that in many ways have a very similar performance style to stand-up. And from this detour we'll bring back an idea around pacing that we can apply to stand-up.

Caroline Goyder, the author of *Gravitas,* is a leading voice coach. She is also a keynote speaker and I have directed Caroline in her own speaking. We originally worked together on a talk

Caroline gave at the London Business Forum in 2016. 'I was in the LSO's rehearsal space, and you talking about referencing the space was such a useful thing because it really grounds the speech. I've used it since in different spaces and there's something very elegant about that. It makes the speech very bespoke to the space and the audience.'

Regarding working the room: 'My teaching had given me a bit of that, because that's what you learn to do as a teacher. [Caroline was a voice coach at the Central School of Speech and Drama.] But as a teacher, it's just totally improvised but my sense is, in stand-up, from what I've learnt from you, it can be a set of very conscious choices that you actually think through in advance. I like the way you say, "If they laugh at this point try this, and if they don't laugh then you can do that instead." It's like you have options at any point. It's very considered but you make it look as if it's improvised.'

Most notably I directed Caroline in a TEDx talk that at the time of writing has received over four million views. This talk was about public speaking so Caroline was telling *and* showing her audience how to speak. There was an added pressure therefore to ensure the talk was itself a good example of speaking! Caroline described her work to me:

> My work is very specifically around voice in the physical sense. Often, it's about helping someone to feel relaxed and confident and to take their time. If I can help them connect their words with their bodies, which is what you would do with an actor, then that brings the speech alive. Most people are highly intellectual in how they approach the speech, even speech writers. Actors really start with the body and then get to the brain afterwards. I'll ask, 'How are you breathing? What are you feeling? What do you want the audience to feel?' That very somatic approach to speech. If you combine the intellectual with the somatic, rather than a talking head, you get a much more powerful and natural human speaker.

We introduced some comic moments to the TEDx talk and often this began with finding the attitude. For example, Caroline had some rather elaborate props made and was feeling self-conscious about using them but was trying to hide this and interact with them well. Rather than hiding the awkwardness, I felt that actually bringing it out and exaggerating it would create some humour. I asked her who had made them and she told me about George, and how while the props were brilliant they were bigger and more striking than she had anticipated.

So rather than taking the props as a given, I had her reference George in the talk. She recalled, 'That was brilliant, bringing in the relationship with George, the maker, and playing with the props being clunky and tricky to work with: "Oh god, I gave this brief to George and this is what he came up with." The humour that you helped me find added a real layer that lifted the talk up a whole couple of notches and I wouldn't have found it on my own.'

But more important than finding some comic moments was bringing stand-up comedy thinking to the entirely straight aspects of the presentation. The first thing I did with Caroline was to go through what she wanted to say and to identify the payoffs. In this case, these are the points that Caroline wants the audience to remember. Once the payoffs have been identified you can then construct the set-ups. Caroline comments on delivering her key points with impact, 'If we hadn't done it, the speech at TEDx would have been so different and so less impactful. You just helped me dial up important moments. There was something about working in a stand-up way, that gave me a structure, a grammar for setting things up properly in a way that would get a result, and it not just being luck.'

'Dialling up important moments' is a good way of putting it. In comedy, they would usually be the 'ha-ha' moments, but in a talk they are the 'ah ha' moments you want to land with impact. Caroline goes on, 'And finding those was just so powerful. It really gave me so much confidence knowing where those moments were. It was your insights from stand-up around how to set it up and how to punch it out, that were completely transformative.'

I was particularly keen that the talk would end on a surprise. Caroline had been talking about the importance of pauses and taking breaths. Knowing that TED talks often thrive on the counter-intuitive, it suddenly struck me that *speaking is all about knowing when to close your mouth*. Caroline said that left her to her own devices, 'I wouldn't have got to it in such a concise way and I wouldn't have delivered it with such *kapow*, with such punch. If it weren't for nailing that punchline, it wouldn't have half the views it's got.'

As stand-up comedians have discovered the benefits of having a director, so too, in effect, have speakers in other contexts. Caroline agreed that this is the case: 'Increasingly people recognize that. People have personal trainers, don't they? I had a call this morning from someone who's director general, is doing lots of speaking and he recognizes that he needs some help to lift it to the next level. I think, increasingly in business, people are recognizing that if you want to be a better speaker you can't do it on your own, you need someone else with an outside eye and an outside ear, who can get you out of your bad habits.' I asked Caroline to give an example of a typical bad habit, and she picked something that, as we have seen, new stand-up comics often struggle with too: talking too fast. Caroline says:

> Often when people are going really fast, they're going at the speed of their thoughts. If you want someone to slow down, first you just understand that all speech is out-breath, that's really important. And then by default, your pauses are on an in-breath. Sometimes I get people to sing their lines, because when we sing, we pause and we breath – we use the breath. It's just understanding how voice and breath work and getting someone to see that *thought* is really connected to *breath*: 'Now I'm breathing in, I'm taking in a thought, now I'm breathing out and speaking, and I'm sending that thought to my audience. Now I'm breathing in, I'm taking in my next thought' and so on. It takes them a while to get that very physical process – it's like learning to drive and at first, it's a bit clunky. If they practice, in the end they can walk out on stage and make it look like they're talking to their oldest friends at the pub. I guess some stand-up comedians do it naturally, but for people who don't, and there's lots of people who don't, that's a really useful thing to learn.

It's striking Caroline made that analogy: It's like you're talking to friends in a pub, as that's precisely the delivery that I'm trying to get stand-up comedians to arrive at. In the end, the audience have no clue that there was any coaching or directing. It just looks like the most natural thing in the world. Caroline agrees: 'Exactly and it's funny because that's what you did with me. I was talking to a client today and he was saying, "We can talk about the speech writers but we can't talk about what *you* do." I said, "Yes, I know I'm invisible.

That's my job." And it's that thing, if I've done my job well, you won't even notice there's been any coaching at all.'

And it's the same with directing stand-up comedy, in the end it should be invisible. Caroline adds: 'And it's lovely, isn't it? Because the gift for the coach is seeing that person perform. I had a client saying, "I've felt ten foot taller and that's what you did with me. I felt so much more empowered on stage because I had a plan." *Your* art is that you make me feel clever! That's the art, isn't it? And it's very clever to do that, because actually you gave most of those ideas but you made me feel like *I'd* come up with them.'

# Act-outs

Let's return to the world of stand-up with *act-outs*. Whenever you have presented the audience with a comic idea, situation or a moment in a story, you can get further laughs by *acting it out*. Mr Cee refers to this as 'tell, then show'. Act-outs really bring stand-up to life. Oliver Double doesn't use the term *act-out* in his seminal book *Getting the Joke*; instead, he uses his own phrase, 'instant character'. He describes the process: 'The kind of acting I'm talking about involves an instant transition from narrator to character achieved through tone of voice, posture or facial expression. ... Even animals and inanimate objects can be characterized. This is an incredibly common mode of performance in stand-up, and most comedians use it in their acts. Eddie Izzard calls it "the motherlode."'[1]

While he used his own phrase in his book, Oliver is familiar with the term *act-out*: 'Yes, *act-out* has become a much more accepted phrase now. I remember in 2000 [comics saying] they didn't have a word for it then, but it has become much more normal now.' Geoff Whiting, on the other hand, has long been familiar with the term: '"Act-outs" has been in use for at least twenty years. I'm sure of it. I heard it when I started.' This underscores the gradual, localized evolution of the language of stand-up.

Mr Cee described how new acts can be uncomfortable with act-outs: 'Some people, at first are not willing to do act-outs. They feel that it's not them. That's just another level of the fear of doing stand-up. For the average Joe, their worst fear is public speaking. For some comedians, their worst fear is trying to act or do a different voice. In the same way, you show somebody who's got fear of public speaking that stand-up is just a conversation, then you show the stand-up that an act-out is just a snapshot of your mind. There's no wrong way you can do it because the audience would accept whatever you deliver.'

Sometimes stand-ups have got wonderful physicality, and they make a big performance of their act-out. Often, however, it's quite casually done. Act-outs can be just action, sometimes just a single voice, but act-outs often feature two sides of a dialogue. This can create a natural set-up/payoff rhythm where the first speaker says the set-up and the second the payoff. You don't need lots of 'he saids' and 'she saids', and you don't need to be good at voices although, if you are, that's great. It's just about giving your audience two different attitudes. There are many ways of approaching this in a performance, but a simple way of differentiating one character from the other is with a change of eyeline. Character A looks to the left, Character B to the right, and when it's you talking to the audience; you do so down the middle. However you do it, aim to make it look casual.

Oliver went on, 'I think that's my favourite type of stand-up, where somebody's describing some experience or fantastical idea and they're acting it out. When that's done really well it's so vivid. It's just one person on stage doing [the whole scene] in collaboration with the collective imagination of the audience.' Crucially the comic doesn't disappear into the character. The audience simultaneously sees the stand-up and the character; it is the stand-up's take on the character: 'It's all to do with layering. For example, when you see Richard Pryor being a deer, the point isn't that he looks exactly like a deer, it's that you can see Pryor *and* the deer. I think the casualness is part of that; it's being able to slip without any apparent effort or pre-planning into these vivid characterizations. It's still vivid but with the illusion of spontaneity as well.'

Mr Cee talked about how enjoyable act-outs are: 'The act-out becomes the fun part of the conversation for both the audience and the person delivering it. As an act, those are the moments you look forward to. Not just the words of the punchline but that moment where you *show* people a little bit of your world.' Mr Cee straddles the mainstream comedy circuit and also the black circuit. Comics on the black circuit are taking act-outs one step further. 'In White Yardie's last show, he *tells you* then he says he's going to *show you* and the curtain goes up, and on-stage actors will enact what he's talking about, *but* he's the only voice you hear. Which is a fantastic way of doing it. He's brought something new into the game. It does detract from the stand-up as a solo artist showing you through words and mimicry alone, but he's taking it to another dimension. It'll be interesting to see whether others will take that new vision on board.'

## Directing stand-up like a play

Having begun this chapter by arguing that stand-up performance cannot be directed like a play performance, which is typically the case, here is an unusual example where a director did just that! Sam Miller directed Kate Smurthwaite in her stand-up show *My Professional Opinion*.

For him it was quite a new experience to work with somebody who had twelve pages of notes rather than a script. At the same time, he really did treat it like a theatre show. When he directed me, he made me do the whole show and pretty much sat there with a megaphone going, 'Bigger. Louder. More, more. Up, up!' And that show won an award, so I can't knock it! The first three days that I did the show in Edinburgh he was at the back of the room, waving his arms, kind of indicating, 'Go louder, go bigger. Calm this down.' He was air traffic controlling the whole show from the back of the room. Then once he was happy with it, he cleared off back to London. [As a director] I've never gone quite that far myself but it's definitely affected how I direct other people. I'll think, 'Hold on a minute, I'm here to direct' and it's actually fine to shout 'Hold on, stop. In this bit, you're trying to impersonate yourself, aren't you? Okay. So, let's do a real impersonation, let's make it big. Let's really do an exaggeration of yourself.' Or, 'Hold on a minute, this bit is supposed to be quiet, let's really take it down, let's make everybody lean in.' Actually, as a performer I might have thought [this kind of directing] would be off-putting but it isn't, it's great. You want someone to stop you and say, 'Right. Let's try this bit again and let's get it right.'

# ACT 3

# Full-length shows and theatre

# 11

# Developing and structuring full-length shows

Club gigs range from five-minute open spots to ten minutes paid or unpaid; the paid slots tend to be, in unusual cases, fifteen minutes, and more commonly twenty minutes (which can be opening, middle and sometimes closing) and then thirty or forty minutes to close. A full-length show is typically one hour but can be longer: for example, ninety minutes with an interval for a touring show, and in some cases even longer. (Ken Dodd being a notorious example with him describing his audiences as 'hostages'.)

At the Edinburgh Fringe, comedy shows are mostly an hour – but in practice, they are not literally sixty minutes. Phil Nichol states: 'When I'm directing someone, I say, "you should be coming off stage at fifty-two-and-a-half minutes." It's almost scientific. I'm working with Patrick Monahan and I've had him finish his shows at that point and he's starting to see the benefit. If you can't tell a story in that time, then you've got too much. Fifty-five minutes is the absolute most you should do.'

Whatever the length, the fundamental points in this section apply to any festival, touring show or even TV special, but we will focus on Edinburgh, the pre-eminent festival for comedy globally. Discussing the leap from a club set to an Edinburgh show, Kate Smurthwaite told me:

> If you're just doing twenty minutes, or less in some clubs, you don't need to give people a break. People can laugh continuously for twenty minutes. But you can't expect people to laugh for a whole hour, which is why a *show* needs some kind of shape. There

has to be a sad bit or a weird bit or a sing-along bit. Something
has to happen that isn't just punchline, punchline, punchline.
I'm put in mind of Alan Cochrane's lovely show *Comedy with
Sad Bits*. Sometimes it's nice to have a moment of poignancy or
honesty.

Geoff Whiting said of the Edinburgh Fringe:

What you do at Edinburgh needs to be completely different
[from a club gig]. I would never do a club set at Edinburgh: It
would be a waste of time. It's not what the audience or the critics
expect. They expect a narrative or some revelation about your
life or at least a theme. A professional club comic, a friend of
mine, complained to me that he'd done a fantastic Edinburgh
show that had got a one-star review. I asked, 'What was the show
about?' He said 'It wasn't about anything. It was an hour of my
best material.' I said, 'That's why you got a one-star review.' You
almost need two sets: an Edinburgh set and a club set. If you
look at someone like Phil Nichol or Brendan Burns, they can
do a club set and they can do an Edinburgh show. A complete
comic can do that. Many an act's whole career has turned on the
Edinburgh Festival, like Micky Flanagan and Jason Manford. I
talk to acts a lot about Edinburgh; when to go, whether to go.
Because if acts go too early, if they go after a year say or eighteen
months, they're almost never ready.

Rather than leaping too soon to a festival 'hour', a graduated
approach is to start with a three-hander show where each act
does approximately fifteen minutes, and they rotate the compèring
duties. Then from there are the two-hander and – if the act is
ready – the solo show. With his character Wisebowm, Steve Whiteley
jumped to doing an Edinburgh solo hour quickly on the back of
an encouraging first year on the London new act circuit. This put
Steve into the category of someone who technically went too early:
'I went into the whole process completely naively. I applied and my
show got accepted. I started running the show in April [the Fringe
is in August], having done the first gig in April the year before. I was
under tremendous pressure trying to put a show together, and doing
fifty minutes in my first year. But I don't regret that because it has
led to where I am now.' For new acts, Edinburgh is always a massive

(and often cripplingly expensive and emotionally draining) learning experience. For Steve, it was an eye-opener being out of the London circuit: 'You've got people coming from all over the UK and the world. So, you have to find ways to present your material that are going to connect with all kinds of people. Performing in Edinburgh opens you up to that.' Another benefit of the Fringe is being able to get a show in front of audiences every day for almost a month. Steve recalled, 'I was constantly adjusting the material based on where I was getting laughs. Sometimes that would change depending on the audience, but I would scrap bits where I was consistently not getting laughs. And I'd ad-lib new jokes every day and the best ones stayed in. You're writing it on the fly. It wasn't until the last three days [of his first Fringe] that I felt I had a finished show. Until then it was work in progress.'

Many acts see Edinburgh in these terms; by the end of the run, you will have a show. It's then a case of taking it on tour and perhaps bringing it back the following year as Steve is doing: 'I've done over a hundred gigs now. I feel much more confident. I'm not going into the unknown. I know the character works. The other big change is, since last year, building up the music aspect, we're turning it into a musical, and that's going to be a massive shift in the whole energy of the show.'

While many people do bring shows back to Edinburgh, perhaps in a revamped version like Steve, it's still the case that most acts go up with an entirely new show. John Gordillo, speaking as a director and a comic, feels that, 'One of the reasons why we have a creatively healthy and rich circuit is because Edinburgh asks a whole bunch of us to come up with something new every year.' The TV special, for the likes of Netflix, also forces comics to create new shows, because once you've filmed your material – and 'burned it' – you need to throw it away.

These kinds of American stand-up specials don't necessarily have such a focus on theme or narrative as Edinburgh shows. John Gordillo commented:

You can see shows where you say: 'That's a really good story that you told. It's a great movie.' But I think the stand-up shows that I find the most satisfying involve people without a theme. They are just being funny. The people who I think are really masterful at this, and who I really enjoy, are mostly American. I just enjoy their worldview. Bill Burr for instance. Then you get to Jerry Seinfeld. He's one of the greatest. Seeing him do his collection of 20 years of jokes at the London Palladium when he was retiring them [*I'm Saying This For the Last Time*], I thought 'There's not a single thing that connects these jokes but the vision that he puts forward.' He's always had this sort of Zen Buddhist approach to comedy where there's something sublime and much bigger than anything in any single observation. There's a real gentle, master worldview coming through. There's something very redemptive that comes out of it.

Whether or not there's an explicit narrative or theme, with festival shows and TV stand-up specials, there does tend to be an expectation that the show will have richer content than a comedy club set. Moreover, doing a full-length show can give the comic licence to tackle weightier topics than in the average comedy club. Oliver Double observed: 'Comedy can be deep and really funny at the same time. I think what's happened since I wrote the first edition of *Getting the Joke*, is that the longer conceptual shows have become much more normal.'

For a lot of acts, the festival show is the first time they work with a director. The leap from the comedy club circuit to a festival show is a significant one and it's here that a director is particularly useful. For Geoff Whiting, 'There are a lot of comedians who are not necessarily good at structuring one hour because it's not something you have to do in a club. Also, there's a narrative arc in an Edinburgh show which you don't have in twenty minutes. The director can help with getting it right.'

A question I always ask at the outset is 'Why are you saying all this?' Typically, an act might respond: 'To make people laugh and be entertained.' Then I drill down: 'But if we're going to make them sit there for an hour and listen to you, at the end they've got to go away feeling like you've said something. So, what is that?' Even with a whimsical show something can be found. For example, Dec Munro is directing Alisdair Beckett-King's 2017 Edinburgh show *The Alisdair Beckett-King Mysteries*. He told me, 'If you were doing a one-line elevator pitch, it's essentially a defence of whimsy at a point in the world where people might say that whimsy isn't the most important or useful thing.' This also addresses another question that's worth asking: 'Why now?' Dec continued, 'Yes, and I think that is incredibly important. "Why do you need to talk about this subject at this time? Why is it important to you and why is it important to us? Why should anybody care?"'

# The director as dramaturg

John Gordillo directed Reginald D. Hunter in his Perrier-nominated 2003 Edinburgh show: 'A person comes to you and says, "Here are all my bits." And you're listening and thinking: "Okay what's that *really* about?" Eventually you can distil that into a simple, "Oh, it's really about *that*." That's their beef. In Reg's case, he had a brilliant title, *White Women*. I did two or three sessions of sitting down with him, saying: "I want all your experiences, thoughts and feelings about white women." What emerged, which was narratively very satisfying in the show, is that actually *it wasn't* about white women. It was actually about the power of image and perception.' Once this had been established, they became aware that a lot of Hunter's existing material could be adapted to fit the theme: 'On the surface it didn't seem to be about that, but with a little work it could be brought into it. It could be *angled*.'

When stand-up Eleanor Conway, a *rebel sensualist*, began developing her confessional Edinburgh 2016/17 and touring show *Walk of Shame*, about her days of drinking, drug taking and partying, she first worked with John Gordillo before subsequently working with me. She discussed with me her time working with John: 'We spent a lot of time together, probably October 2015 to about March/April 2016. I got loads out of that. He is always about the bigger picture. I showed him five minutes of stand-up. From that, he'd ask, "What does that say about you?" I'd say, "It's just a dick joke." "Yes, but what does this say about you and your approach to men?" That elevated it, hopefully, a little bit.' John Gordillo described his approach:

I'll ask them everything about what they think around the subject. I am more than happy just listening and asking and interrogating everything to get a sense of what the mission of the project is. First of all, I think you need to try and get in the head and shoes of the person. What is it that they are trying to do? So, you can really get a sense of what their ambition is for it, and what their intention is. From there you may want to question some of those ambitions: 'Hang on have you thought about this?' With me, I just feel like I'm just trying to apply my most pedantic judgement to the question that's in front of me.

Eleanor Conway expands on the process she went through with John:

I'd go to his place, for four to six hours sometimes. We'd just talk, talk and talk. He would help me get under the hood of it. He was constantly asking questions. He's just really good. No subject is out of bounds. We talked about porn, drugs, addiction, really honest, gritty, stuff in order to try and find out what was interesting about it. I'd record the session. Then I would listen back and transcribe the main points. Usually, I realized that my ego was taking over in those sessions and I was talking over John! He would give me good little slivers of ideas that I would completely miss in the session, and that I would pick up after I had listened to the recording. Over time, hopefully, I have become more collaborative.

John Gordillo commented that, like me, he 'always advises people to record the sessions. When you're in the room with someone you don't hear everything.' Eleanor described what she got out of the process: 'Working with John, he taught me a lot about the bigger idea; what is the show about? This idea of condensing the show into one line. What's *Walk of Shame* about? It's about the extremes I go to in life. That's pretty much what it's about.'

At the time of writing, John Gordillo is directing Phil Nichol's 2017 Edinburgh show. Phil described the show: 'I'm writing a show about the inability to admit you're wrong. I've been going through micro and macro, finding everything from spelling "you're" without an apostrophe – the show is called *Your Wrong* – everything from there up to Brexit and Trump. It's all knee-jerk, "I'm right, you're wrong" bullshit because who's going to decide what's right and wrong anymore?' Having established the theme, Phil next asks himself:

'Okay, what stories do I have that are in the ballpark but not on topic?' For example, I can tell a story about having a lisp and go,

'When I grew up I had a lisp and a stutter.' I could make that into how people treated me as if I'm an idiot and I'm wrong. Then my political point would be: We shouldn't just degrade thinkers because they don't *appear* as smart. A tribesman in the woods in the Amazon may not appear smart compared to us because he doesn't know what a phone is, but he may be far wiser. So, I'm going from me having a stutter and a lisp, back to my point.

Director John Gordillo recalled that when Phil came to him, 'he had a bunch of stories and they would seem to me to be nominally on the theme of right and wrong. Then I realized, "Oh, this is about certainty, you just don't trust certainty." *That* can be the attack.' Kate Smurthwaite has an intriguing exercise to uncover what points a comic wants to make:

I say, 'Go away and write your show as a ten-minute TED talk.' It's really interesting when you see that from, for example, a drag queen. You might think of it as a silly over-the-top show – he's going to be in a wig and too much makeup and taunting people – but actually, when you see it as a TED talk, there *is* something they want to say. And [as director] you say, 'This is beautiful. I really want you to be able to say *this* much more than just write a whole string of jokes that will definitely last an hour.' You do come away from a great show feeling like something has been said. Not necessarily that they provide all the answers but something about the way you see the world has shifted a little bit.

Chris Rock employs this strategy of working out what he wants to say first and only then moves on to working out how to make it funny.[1] When we spoke, Ahir Shah told me he recognizes this approach: 'With my director, in the first stage, we'll be exploring the general themes, the topics I want to talk about and the ideas that I have.' But he added, 'Sometimes the genesis of a particular piece [within a show] *will* be a joke. It anchors it in my head, when you come up with this particular line that's going to be the biggest laugh point on an idea. Now I have that nugget I can start building around it.'

Samantha Baines's 2017 Edinburgh show, while being primarily about three brilliant and forgotten women of science, has a strand that is about the death of her father; indeed, it ends rather poignantly where she says, in reference to the lost women of science she has uncovered *and* her father: 'If someone is remembered they are not really lost.' It's a great ending. A problem with this is there have been several shows that have explored this pivotal life event, and the 'dead dad' show has become something of a genre (lampooned by Stewart Lee no less). To address this, I suggested that the material where she referenced her new husband was developed and foregrounded more, and to bring in some references to trying *not* to talk about Brian Cox. (Her previous year's show had been all about Cox.) Then the show became about, as Samantha put it, 'three brilliant women and three alright men.' Which gave the show a neat balance and avoided too much focus on the more familiar topic of the loss of a father.

As in this case, part of the director's input can be an awareness of trends and previous shows that have a bearing on the current one. Dec Munro commented, 'That's such a good example of this because otherwise she may well end up with a show that is dominated to a significant extent by that topic. It's such an important thing in her life, and that's out of your control, but it's vital to flag it up. It is so sad that the "dead dad" show has become a genre and it has become a thing that's almost seen as hack. That's really desperately sad: "Oh not another person talking about their entire world being ripped apart."' He went on:

> A director can be useful simply to say, 'You know what? I've seen this before.' It's important to be aware of themes that have developed – you can say, for example, in 2015, 2016 to a degree, shows exploring mental health were big in Edinburgh. Bridget Christie joked about this after she won the Edinburgh prize: She said, well, she cured feminism, as a result [people] couldn't talk about feminism in the future. I think it is worth being aware of the last five, six, seven years' worth of themes, if only so that you can know that one of the first things a reviewer, albeit a lazy reviewer, might do is immediately compare shows to previous ones with similar themes.

# Structuring shows

When I directed Katia Kvinge's 2016 Edinburgh show *Squirrel*, after the dramaturgical phase, we ended up with two very distinct stacks of material for the show. One was a series of cartoonish character *set pieces* and the other was a selection of heartfelt true stories. The challenge was reconciling the two.

When I say 'stacks' of material, I mean it quite literally. I like to use index cards. Each piece of material is summarized on a card, and we spread all the cards across a long table. Each card has a title to remind us what the bit is – it could be a gag, a story (or a segment of a story), something musical, something physical (and Katia's show combined all these elements). I might take this further with a star system – one, two or three stars for how strong we judge each piece to be. We can then shift the show around to our heart's content, discussing the various implications of each order.

Katia remembers, 'I found it really helpful, writing on the cue cards. Just saying, "Let's just get every joke down on a card" and then seeing where they fit.' We ended up with a situation where about half the cards were material that was emphatically *cartoon* in style and the other half were autobiographical and *realist*. For a long time, we had all the autobiographical cards at the top of the table. The idea was that she would introduce herself to the audience before getting down to the show proper which consisted of all her familiar characters, voices and larking about. As there was so much of this material (about a third of the show's content), we came up with the idea that it was an introduction that had gotten wildly out of hand leaving very little time for the actual show itself.

This thought then suggested that the actual show would be comically rushed to try and fit everything into the time remaining. We doggedly worked with this for a long time, and Katia performed preview shows with this structure, but despite liking the concept, in practice it was problematic. For one thing, people coming to see Katia's show expected all the gooning around and were instead met with a lengthy, personal section that then, with a clunking gear change, went into her normal fun style.

At the eleventh hour, the idea occurred to us to *literally* present it as two shows. From then on, at the top Katia told the audience she'd come up with two different shows she could do in Edinburgh that year. Not being able to decide which to do, she had decided to do both. And then throughout the show she jumped from one to another as if switching between channels with a remote, which created sudden switches of mood from serious to trivial and then back again that, in themselves, generated bathos and laughs. And, as discussed in the next chapter, the two came to reference each other, in that the autobiography revealed why she was such a delightful, manic show-off in the other sections.

Another show that had two very different sides to it was Sofie Hagen's award-winning 2015 show *Bubblewrap*. I asked director Dec Munro to say, in a line, what the show was about. He responded: 'Mental health and Westlife'. He went on, 'At that time mental health was something that not so many comedians were yet talking about. It felt like 2015 was very much the year that people started to talk about it in comedy. Sofie wanted to talk about mental health, but I think she realized very quickly that a show solely focusing on it is difficult to pull off.' She also had an extraordinary story to tell:

> She was voted the top Westlife fan in Denmark! She'd had battles with people as to how much she knew about them. She'd written three hundred plus erotic stories about Westlife between the ages of twelve and fourteen. A few are still on the internet. They are highly erotic fan fiction, and they're very, very funny. If you create a show around somebody's somewhat obsessive interest in something, whether it be football or music or whatever, everybody in the world could identify with it. Then she realized that it would be better if the mental health angle wasn't even something that you really saw until about twenty minutes into the show.

The show ended up in the opposite configuration to how we originally had Katia's show. Where we had a long section of serious material and then flipped to the absurdist content (which is bathos), *Bubblewrap* flips the other way (which is pathos!). Dec went on:

> The show has one pivotal moment, where she goes from talking about Westlife and her somewhat obsessive behaviour towards them, all of which is incredibly funny in retrospect, to how alongside that were certain mental health issues that she was living with and dealing with in a very impressive way. There's a deliberately harsh cut in the show, where you suddenly see that the stuff she's been talking about has this undertone of mental ill health. She then starts to talk about mental health and by that point, as an audience member, you're fully invested – I think it allows you to go along for the rest of the ride.

With Katia's *Squirrel*, the content of the autobiographical 'show' had a natural order to it and we decided to stick with a broadly chronological unfolding. The other 'show' of skits and impressions and games could go in almost any order, so the sequencing here was guided by how strong each bit was – the basic consideration is needing to start and end well, and then within that making sure there is an escalation in how the material unfolds. Put simply: You wouldn't want anything massively outlandish near the start (and Katia certainly had some rather outlandish material) as it'd give you nowhere to build to and later material would seem anti-climactic.

The process of shifting material around according to how strong it appears to be, and then justifying why it's in that order, is a common strategy with stand-up shows. Indeed, with the less narrative-driven US stand-up specials, the 'set-piece' process is very much the method of structuring the material. Once the material has been put into a sequence, some linking and framing often needs to be written. Kate Smurthwaite finds that this material can have a value of its own:

> Sometimes when I start to write the structural bits they become the best bit of the show. and you end up dropping what you thought were your favourite jokes. It's like when movie directors make one scene, then build a whole movie and end up dropping the original scene because it just isn't the best bit anymore.

Kate references movies here. In a similar way, I often think of a stand-up show as being like a sitcom. When I started working with Steve Whiteley as director of Wisebowm, the show was a compilation of comic rhymes and raps that had been working on the circuit plus semi-improvised spoken introductions. My first concern was fleshing out the world of the character more and the people around him. It is all too easy to have a character that exists in a vacuum. Many more possibilities open up when you begin to construct a world of characters around them. Steve recalled:

> I think that helped trying to understand who the character was. Once the world started to develop, I found it easy to write the material and I had a much clearer focus on who he was. Suddenly the character had this whole world, and it was almost like a sitcom, with a beginning, middle and an end. I actually did a sitcom

course with you five years ago but completely forgot about that stuff when writing the show, because it was a completely different beast! But when you saw it, you said 'Oh we'll structure it like a sitcom', and it made complete sense, and it helped me then to go away and write it. And I think from the audience perspective it's much more engaging. I was going to just introduce myself as a comedy rapper and each rap would have an intro and that was it. Suddenly, it's gone from that to this whole world.

I find that a lot of concepts from the world of sitcom can be applied to any stand-up show, and not just narrative shows. One concept from sitcom that is useful is the idea of *set pieces*. Here's Graham Linehan, interviewed in *Mustard Mag* with some advice for aspiring sitcom writers: 'Create two or three big set pieces – e.g. something like Father Ted's Hitler moustache scene. Two or three moments that you're either working towards or writing about the repercussions. Then just make sure you've got lots of nice little gags connecting them up.'[2] As a director, Phil Nichol identifies set pieces, those stand-out bits of material that an act has that are striking in some way and structures the show around them:

A strong show will have five set pieces and a really strong show will have seven to nine. Some are bigger than others. A set piece can be three lines with a wicked punchline. A set piece could also be a song. I say, 'Figure out what your set pieces are and then we work towards strengthening them.' I see it almost like a tent. You have your strongest set piece holding the whole thing up. Because if you know you are heading towards that, as a performer you're excited about it. The audience will also be drawn along. The audience wants to be put at ease that you know where this is going even if it seems scattershot and random. Every time you get to a set piece they'll go, 'Right, that was satisfying. Next.' Then you can enter into the next chapter from the most obscure angle you want because they start to trust that you always get back to a set piece. I worked with [musical comic] Kirsty Doody last year [2016], it was her first Edinburgh show [*Life Begins at Party*]. She was telling the story of her different parties as she was growing up; teenage parties, parties in your twenties, parties in your thirties. Initially, it was linear, starting from baby parties. It would have been fine, but I asked, 'What's the best party section?' Material-wise it's the twenties, that was the strongest, so we put that first. And then the teenage party became a little bit stronger, so we moved that and put that first. So, once you've got the sections and set pieces, you can move them into almost any order. The story still works, because no one tells a story in a strictly linear fashion.

With more storytelling shows, Phil says once you have your set pieces in place it's a question of 'how you hang the narrative between them'. You construct the telling of the story around this sequence of set pieces. Of course, you're looking for a naturalness or elegance to the structure, but if the show becomes particularly scattered or idiosyncratic, Phil said, 'You can laugh at the *way* you're telling it as much as *what* you're telling.'

He went on: 'Ideally, you should be able to get it tight enough that it's all jokes and set pieces. That's what you're aiming for, but to write that in a year is quite difficult. You need to work on the set pieces and the shape of the show first and *then* find the way of telling the story. Josh Howie wrote a show called *Aids: A Survivor's Story* [which Phil helped him with], which was *set-up, joke, set-up, joke, set-up, joke* for the entire thing and it told a story.'

# The three-act structure and plot lines

Two major concepts from sitcom plotting (and indeed other kinds of narratives) that I apply to stand-up shows are the three-act structure and multiple plotlines that unfold in parallel and ultimately collide. First, the three acts.

- *Act 1* – setting up the show, introducing the comic and the themes/subject matter and ending with a dilemma, challenge or problem of some kind (set-up, reveal);
- *Act 2* – developing and deepening these themes and complicating the dilemma or challenge (escalation);
- *Act 3* – rounding the show off and resolving the dilemma or challenge or not (payoff).

Phil Nichol again: 'I don't actually think in terms of three acts, but I do think stories fall into that pattern. You can see that in most films.

I've been writing screenplays now for a few years, sold a couple. With screenwriting, they always tell you that tone is the most important thing. Someone reading a script, within the first three pages, if the tone isn't set, they won't read it. I think it's the same with a theatre piece or a stand-up show. If it's convoluted within the first three minutes, the audience is thinking, "Oh God this is going to be horrible." You need to make it so clear and concise at the beginning. Making a show run to a structure alleviates any stress from the audience.'

Turning to the plot lines; if you had, for example, three plot lines the A plot would be the main thrust of the show, the B plot a secondary strand and the C plot a lesser strand. The A plot has the lion's share of the show's running time, the B plot a lower amount and the C plot (etc.) a relatively small amount of time. The plots develop incrementally through the show, with the comic shifting focus from one to another. As in sitcom, the classic approach to resolving the show is to have all three plot strands colliding.

For example, I directed Paul McMullan in his 2016 Edinburgh stand-up show at Pleasance Courtyard *Alcopop*. The story of his alcoholism and recovery, the A plot, was naturally just that – the title being a punning reference to him having been an alcoholic father. There was also a strong strand relating to relationships which while it was an inseparable part of the main story, we looked on as the B plot. This approach was helpful in shaping the story as we could track the development of the B plot separately from the A plot. When we first met (quite a way into the process), I suggested the show needed a C plot – something not apparently related to the main strands. For some reason, as an example, I suggested 'dogs'. Paul responded to this random suggestion immediately – his sons had wanted a dog and he didn't like dogs. The dog story became the C plot and we engineered it so that all three plots collided at the end in classic sitcom style.

John Gordillo will work with these kinds of structural devices but does not let them dominate: 'I would use things like a three-act structure or A plot, B plot. But because in stand-up the will and the whim of the performer are what matters, it's important that the structure isn't too rigid. It needs to have a feeling of fluidity. So, you want to be as subservient, or apparently subservient, to the seemingly improvised, caught-in-the-moment, nature of the performance as possible.'

And when I work in this way, although we've established the structure, in the end, the audience won't see it. Ultimately, the comedian and I will have forgotten it as well. John Gordillo agreed: 'Yes, I don't want to see it either. I want to sit there and think, "How did we get there?" Absolutely, I want to forget all of it.' The structure is just the scaffolding that's there for a while, and then we can take it down.

John went on, 'It's always about trying to create a non-intellectual experience because it's a gut reaction, laughter. It's about connecting emotionally. Whatever you come to me with, absolutely we are looking to sharpen the content, to make sure that it's coherent and consistent, and that there's development and growth, that there's narrative. But you know, it's just about: Does it feel right? The kind of comedy I like the most is about divulging and is about exposure, and it's about sharing. It's about intimacy.'

# Chronology

With storytelling or autobiographical shows there are the issues of chronology, with a straight chronological telling often not being the most effective way of a story unfolding. Few people telling a story of several years of their life socially would stick rigidly to the chronological unfolding. For one thing, a very common starting point would be *the present moment*: Why the story comes to mind now. John Gordillo again:

> You've got to tell the story of you *now* first, and you've really got to justify why you're going into the past. Stand-up is a present-tense medium, the whole point is the stuff is happening now or consuming you here and now. That is one of the beauties of it. Every now and then, someone comes along, and they present their show to me: '*And I did this, and I did that.*' And I'm always asking, 'Why do I care when I don't even know you?' I don't care what happened to you when you were young. What I need to know is why you're fucked up about this *now*? What's happening *now* to justify this? 'This just happened the other day.' Maybe yesterday. Everything is as close as possible. As soon as you tell me it was a couple of years ago, I say, 'Really? Why are you telling me then?' It must come out of the present circumstance.

If a chronological telling is X/Y/Z, an alternative might be Z/X/Y where we begin with the *now* and go back in time to discover the inciting incidents. Another structural trick is to embed one strand within another. So instead of the two strands running one after the other, X/Y (now/then), you have X/Y/X (now/then/now). Phil Nichol took this kind of approach in his show *The Weary Land*: 'I started [the show] by recalling a poem I'd written under a moment of stress, and got to the point where I was about to read the poem. Then I say, "But before I do that, I'll explain how I got there," and I go all the way back to the beginning of my life, which is almost film-like. It worked for that story. I needed to tell the audience all of this stuff. [At the end] I come back to the poem, and it's almost as if they've forgotten all about it and they go, "Oh, what? Oh my God," which gives the poem the value that it needs. The reason for doing the show is to read the poem.'

# Endings

Ahir Shah had a striking metaphor for how he structures his shows and how it builds to the ending:

> I think one of the finest structural comedians is Daniel Kitson. I remember seeing his show *It's the Fireworks Talking* [Edinburgh Fringe 2007], where everything was brought together at the end and the payoff was so severe and unexpected. I subsequently tried to do that kind of thing in my shows. It's almost like at the beginning I've got an empty bag, and you watch me as I'm putting things into that bag for an hour, and keep putting in and keep putting in. And then at the end I say to you, 'Go on pick up the bag.' You pick it up and you go, 'Crap, I had no idea it was going to be that heavy. When did all of this happen?' You can utilize structure and bring stuff together in that way in order to deliver real impact at the end of an hour and that's what I'm interested in.

For example, in his current show *Control*, the themes of visiting Nando's as a vegetarian, losing pub arguments and *off milk* build to an ending where, as he says, 'I'm discussing the entire state of the

Western world at that moment.' Phil Nichol finds the ending often emerges during the process:

> After a certain point, you start to be able to ask, 'What's the end, what are you saying?' Often with me, the end doesn't come along till quite late and then you have to go back and fix everything to make the end work. A lot of Edinburgh shows have [followed] a trend to leave the crying scenes until the end. Everyone cries, then they all feel better about it. It's effective, and that's why people do it. Audiences love it but I can see it coming a mile away. I'd rather you play with the form, play with the structure and not necessarily have that be the climax of the piece.

How a show ends colours how the audience feels about the whole experience. A show that has so far felt 'okay' as it's in progress can be redeemed by a brilliant ending, leaving the audience with the overall impression that the show was brilliant. And the reverse is true too: a brilliant show will be greatly diminished by an 'okay' ending. Here are some kinds of endings that I always have in mind:

1  The primary one is probably the *callback*, a classic device where something from earlier is unexpectedly brought back in a new context.

2  There is also the *false dawn* – everything seems resolved or back to normal but in the end it turns out not to be.

3  A *call-to-action* is another effective ending. This is where the performer wants the audience to now go ahead and do something. For example, I suggested this ending for Samantha Baines's forgotten women of science show. The call to action being: *go out and tell everyone about these women.*

4  I do enjoy a *meta-ending*. Metacomedy is where you draw attention to the process for comic effect. I elaborate on this in the next paragraph.

5  A particularly good ending is what I term the *QED* ending, which is where you say what you have proved or established through the show. It can be genuine or facetious. You can look at a nearly finished show and ask yourself: What have I proved through all this? I have known shows (and sets)

arrive at a satisfying and funny ending that seems like the
whole show was constructed to make that point, but in fact,
it was discovered late in the day.

To return to the meta-ending, a memorable example came in a Sean
Lock show I saw at the Edinburgh Fringe in the Pleasance (2007)
where, right at the end of the show, he did a routine that ended on
a so-so laugh – and then said that was meant to be his big laugh
to end on. As it wasn't a big enough laugh he couldn't, with his
professional pride intact, go off. So now he was in the position of
having to generate a laugh from nothing that would be big enough
to go off on. Of course, we the audience were all falling about. And
he picked one of the laughs and said, 'that'll do' – and went off. I
suspect this whole ending was ad-libbed one night and then stayed
in. This can't be precisely scripted, but with a clear sense of what
the game is, it can be played with variations show after show.

# 12

# Vulnerability and pain in stand-up shows

Stand-up shows can be purely whimsical or surreal, little touching on the personal life of the comic. At the other extreme, the stand-up will share intimate, painful truths and confessions. In this chapter we look more closely at highly personal stand-up shows, exploring the impetus to get personal in the first place, finding the funniness in bleak real-life situations and the particular structural considerations of including very dark or challenging material. The chapter ends by exploring the performance and directing of this kind of material.

## Getting personal

When I directed Katia Kvinge, an *innocent creator,* in her 2016 Edinburgh show *Squirrel* at the Gilded Balloon, I was keen to make it more personal. Katia told me, 'In 2014 in my first solo show *Karakters*, I did six or seven characters I'd been doing on the stand-up circuit, at Gaulier's clown school and in improv at Groundlings. Then a year after that I did a show called *140 Karakters* which was me trying to cram in one-hundred-and-forty quick characters into a show.'

I'd seen *140 Karakters* and I felt that while the character performances were great, we the audience learnt nothing about who she is as a person. Katia recalled, 'When I did stand-up as myself at uni, I never liked the whole "baring my soul on stage" and making myself vulnerable to get laughs thing. Whereas when I left and started doing characters I could hide behind a voice or a persona, *and* the jokes I'd been doing as me became funnier said by a character.' For the *Squirrel* show I wanted to see if we could bring back something of her life *alongside* the characters. I felt the audience would appreciate the characters more if they had met the person who was doing them. And it turned out that she had a great bank of engaging, sad and comical true stories about her life, upbringing and in particular her relationships. We then went through a long process of me asking questions and Katia telling me stories. She recalled, 'There were some things where I thought, "Oh my God, I can't believe I'm even sharing this with Chris!"'

Katia went on:

> I remember leaving to go up to the Fringe thinking, 'I just don't want to talk about my own stuff! I just want to do characters!' But I can see with the stuff where you are really being vulnerable, there is more appreciation from the audience. I did have one reviewer say 'oversharing and overbearing!' but for most of the reviewers, and for lots of people who saw the show, it was their favourite aspect of it. They were like, 'Oh, but we really see who you are.' For instance, I just did *Squirrel* in London [summer 2017]. I felt the audience were not on my side in the first five, maybe ten minutes, but then once I'd told them the story about my parents' divorce and being bullied in high school and being a dork, they were like 'We *are* on your side' and then it was way easier for the rest of the hour and I had a really good show. I could see that when I just did characters, [for some of the audience] they'd say 'We don't know who you are, you're just doing some showcase', and that could be annoying for some people, whereas with the *Squirrel* show, it was like 'Yes I do characters, and this is my background, this is *why* I like to do characters.' There was a through line that the audience can get on board with and they can see me as a person.

Regarding these kinds of personal revelations in a show, Simon McBurney said, 'We understand the flow of words as this sea wall against the hurricane of despair that lies behind it. Then, it becomes monstrously funny, and that's key. We have to have a sense of the sea in order to enjoy the security of the sea wall, behind which we can be thrilled with the violence of the waves which should apparently have no effect on us, and be very entertained.' Simon went on:

> Now, I like the term 'stand-up' because it proposes the world's oldest joke. Which is falling over. And, in a sense, in most stand-up, falling over is absolutely part of what is going on. Falling over is about revelation. Falling over reveals the absurd truth of who we are. Change the first 'l' in 'falling' to an 'i' and it's 'failing'; same thing really. Clumsy, inept, vulnerable and idiotic. It peels back pretence, exposes us as an animal who thinks they are more important than we truly are. Dirty laundry hung out to dry. Entrails exposed on the butcher's slab. We the audience gorge on the sudden plunge into that bit of the soul deeply sensitive yet set up to be laughed at, relieved perhaps that it is not us as we plunge into someone else's guts and feast ourselves on the hilarious pretension, stupidity and unattractive emotional digestive system which is actually the source of our humanity. I mean, witness the fact that this year the Edinburgh comedy award was [jointly] won by somebody talking about the most painful break up of his life [John Robins's *The Darkness of Robins* (2017)]. The year that we won the Perrier Award with *More Bigger Snacks Now*, it was 1985, a horrible year really – so our piece was abusive, violent, idiotic – feeding on our lack of money, our sense of being unemployable because we were living on the edge of society, in our hard-to-let council flats, watching friends die from Aids and yet attempting constantly to celebrate in the face of disaster. Looking back, it was an aggressive piece of entertainment. And yes, there was a lot of falling over – a lot – I ate lit cigarettes nicked off the audience. (How weird is that thought today? Would you even find someone with a cigarette?!) We hurt ourselves throughout. But the more we hurt ourselves the louder people laughed.

## Finding the funny in the pain

I spoke with Oliver Double about a show he himself did as a stand-up that was also going into personally and even physically painful areas:

> I did a stand-up show in a theatre in Canterbury called *Break a Leg*. I'd broken my hip and as I was recovering I started to realize

that a lot of the things that I'd been thinking about it were quite funny. Now, the notes from my notebook weren't written as part of a comedy show at all. They were written as a diary for me to make sense of this quite traumatic experience of being put into a geriatric ward at the age of forty-nine, where the youngest of the patients was twenty-five years my senior, in intense pain, unable to walk. Then having to relearn how to walk, being housebound for a month. I was doing drawings and notes as a way of dealing with it, but actually that was the seed of the show.

I asked Oliver how he set about finding funny angles in this quite bleak situation and it was very much a case of applying the kind of thinking we discussed in Chapter 2.

> It starts with observing the world through a comic lens. To give you an example, I was in a ward called 'Cheerful Sparrows'. This tickled me and all the more so because the ward was full of really miserable people. It wasn't a children's ward where you'd understand why they called it that. It was really very conspicuously miserable older people. I suppose the first thing you do is observe that there's a contradiction there. [An incongruity.] And then you ask 'Okay what can I do with that?' So, it's a two-stage process. And I had a PowerPoint [with a photo of the name] so they could see I wasn't making it up. I'd tell them about the miserable people in the ward and I'd say, 'What do you think they chose to call the ward?' Click. 'Cheerful Sparrows.'

Here we see Oliver organizing this into a set-up/payoff rhythm. He begins by giving the audience the picture of how bleak it is and *then* he reveals the name. Whereas when he originally told me this in conversation he gave it away right at the start. But once presenting it in a stand-up context he then hides where it's going: 'It goes back to knowing the value of what you've got. The comic idea is a jewel and you need a good casing for it because otherwise people just don't realize it's the diamond.' Oliver then asked himself why it was called that, 'And I came up with the idea that maybe it was the nurses taking the piss out of the people. They're going, "They're a miserable bunch on that ward. What shall we call it? I know, 'Cheerful Sparrows'. They'll hate it."'

Here Oliver is going back into the past and speculating. Then, as we saw in Chapter 2, one can also extrapolate to the future. Given that they have given this rather absurd avian name for a very bleak setting *now*, you then go into the future and imagine they've got to name a ward and it's even more bleak. It's the most horrific possible ward. You might ask, for example, 'What are they going to call that? "Pleased Puffins?"' Having picked out a detail, Oliver now focused on a story of an upsetting situation that nevertheless had a kernel of humour in it:

> When you're on serious pain killers you get appalling constipation, and I'm in a ward where I can only walk on a zimmer frame and I can't actually go to the toilet by myself. They bring me a commode and there's a sort of thin curtain around me and I'm into this battle of wills between me and my bowel. It's really a very, very humiliating and depressing moment. I remember thinking, 'I'm a university lecturer!' There's something funny there about being an animal and also being a social being, and all your pride and your achievements disappear in the face of a malfunctioning bowel. Then I thought, 'How can I build it into a sequence which is perhaps about three or four minutes?' There's lots of little bits along the way, some of it's a bit corny. There's the occasional line in there where you go, 'Yeah lots of people have said that kind of thing but I know that it's building to something which is probably not generic, which is a very honest bit of self-revelation about me feeling my pride completely evaporating.'

When Oliver was speaking about the scene with the commode I was thinking it's crying out for an act-out and that's exactly how Oliver treats it: 'I perform the nurse and myself and act out the physical geography of the piece.' I asked how he developed the character of the nurse. Was it an impression of the actual person? 'It wasn't necessarily this specific nurse, it was an amalgam of two nurses. And actually, I got to the end and I'd finished and she goes, "Oh well done." I didn't know that was going to be a funny line! That then was a set-up for a joke about basically being praised [for going to the toilet] for the first time since early childhood. It was a sort of defecation humiliation.'

# Structuring painful revelations

I came on board as a second director (see Chapter 3 for the subject of multiple directors) on Eleanor Conway's *Walk of Shame* show as the Edinburgh Fringe 2016 was looming, by which point she had assembled a significant quantity of material from her work with John Gordillo that she had developed in club gigs and previews. A major part of my role was helping her to decide what to include and in what order. Eleanor remembers, 'The process that you and I went on was very important. It was the right combination for me to have that mass load of data, that excavation with John, and then to have you look at the structure.'

Before I met with Eleanor I watched a video of her latest preview and identified all the different elements in the show. As usual, I then gave each bit a title and wrote it onto an index card. When we met at the Picturehouse Central café in Piccadilly Circus, we found a big table and spread all the cards out. Then to construct the show we established three columns: Act 1, Act 2 and Act 3; with, as is typical, Acts 1 and 3 being shorter and Act 2 the meat of it. We were then looking for pieces of material that functioned as set-ups and were introductory, pieces that developed and deepened the dilemmas of the show and pieces that were resolutions or conclusions. And then identified the set pieces.

These naturally fell into the three acts and then it was a case of finding an optimum arrangement and leaving out cards that didn't fit, weren't strong set pieces and didn't advance the narrative. These went on a reserve pile. With Act 2, I was also looking to find a build, an escalation, across the material so that it developed to the stronger and darker stuff, which meant abandoning chronology. The darkest story in the show – one of domestic violence she'd suffered at the hands of a boyfriend she'd followed to South East Asia – was chronologically at the start, which would be too soon.

Phil Nichol described how the audience 'need to understand that it's a comedy show, it's going to be funny and they're safe. So, you need to set up some funny stuff at the beginning, then go back and tell. You have to be very delicate and careful where you place the material, or the audience will sense, "Oh, this is why. That's why she did those jokes at the beginning, she was manipulating us." It has to feel like the story naturally unfolds in that way, that's how you tell it because you need to hold that bit back because it was so uncomfortable you couldn't tell them right away.'

Phil discussed dark subjects in a show: 'It's a sitcom, they're laughing at you. If the stories are dark, you've got to make it so they don't turn off: "Fuck, I can't take this anymore." You need to find stories that make *you* the clown. You're the fall guy in it. So, when Brendan Burns talks about smearing his shit on the wall and calling hookers, I'm sure it wasn't funny for him at the time, but it's funny the way he tells it because he's reflecting upon it and it becomes a sitcom.'

Eleanor Conway recalled, 'By the time I came to you Chris, I was under a lot of pressure. I wasn't sure who to listen to, to be honest. What was interesting that you introduced were the time jumps. That jumping and the element of structure was exciting. Learning that it doesn't have to be chronological and learning those points to jump off and jump back, was great. I think there was a point in our development where I was jumping around a bit too much. But it wasn't that hard to correct that.'

Eleanor went on, 'The problem with going, "Hey guys, can I get everyone's advice," is everyone gives you advice and because you're not solid enough in your own confidence, you listen to everyone. I've got people telling me "Oh no, it *should be* chronological." So, the first three shows or four shows I did at Edinburgh, I scratched what we'd done and went back to the chronological version. It didn't work so I changed it back later in the first week, and it just fit. I wouldn't make that decision again. It was very much about me finding my feet and learning that balance between asking other people for advice and knowing when *not* to listen to that advice.'

## Performing challenging material

I saw an early (non-chronological) show of *Walk of Shame* at the Edinburgh Fringe and felt Eleanor's performance was misfiring. Eleanor recalls, 'I am aware that this is my first show and it's quite a full-on topic to go straight in with. There were a few at the beginning that felt awkward. [Canadian comic] Allyson June Smith gave me some really good advice. She's brilliant. She said, "Eleanor, you need to pretend its sex and it's the first time you're doing it with them." And that was so useful.' When I saw it, there was no sense of seducing the audience! It was very brash and in your face. Some people were engaging with the show nevertheless (and some comics build a career on it!), but many people seemed turned off by this attitude.

From the train, as I left Scotland, I texted Eleanor a flurry of notes about her performance, about the need to lower her defences, show vulnerability and connect with the audience. I next saw the show when Eleanor took it on tour following her ultimately successful Edinburgh run. She'd brought the show to my adopted home town of Stroud and seeing her perform it this time was a revelation. There was a real vulnerability and connection with the audience, and it had the feeling of honest sharing.

This new delivery was partly fostered through a happy accident. Eleanor explained, 'I didn't have a tour support, partly for money reasons but also someone said "You don't want the support to outshine you" and I thought "Oh god, I don't want that to happen!"' So instead of a support act, Eleanor did the first half herself simply talking to the audience, getting to know people and working the room. As an experienced compère, this came naturally to her: 'So at the top I do twenty minutes of banter, then we have a break, and then I do the show. And I think that was absolutely key because I am good at chatting to people and interaction and it helps the audience to know me and each other.'

Like Steve Whiteley, Eleanor is taking an improved version of her last year's show up to Edinburgh: 'I think people get too bound up with this "new show yearly" approach. For me, the minimum objective is to build your audience and develop a show you can tour for eighteen months. It's like an album. I think that era of taking a show up, it being a smash hit and you being on telly by Christmas is a bit over.'

I asked Simon McBurney how he sees the director's role in helping the stand-up mine their personal pain. He responded:

Firstly, directing in the theatre is a kind of fake profession because once the lights are down, the piece is always in the hands of the actors. They are the storytellers. It is their relationship with each other and the audience which is bringing the piece to life. Sometimes the director can get in the way and fuck things up for the actors. So, you are always trying to avoid that I guess. And in stand-up, there is even less need for a 'director'. They are redundant. Really and truly. What are they doing there? So how do we direct a stand-up? Certainly, by not getting in the way. That's for sure. I mean, there is nowhere to tell people to *stand* in stand-up because all they have to do is be there. Behind the microphone. And they are there because they know they will reveal themselves and in so doing reveal something about us, the audience, and in recognizing what makes them 'stand-up' perhaps we recognize ourselves. And so, we laugh. To laugh there has to be a truth. And the best truth, I guess, is that which is true to your own experience. Perhaps – I dunno – perhaps the only function of a director in stand-up is to be able to help something emerge. How do you do that? Fuck. Well you have to listen. You have to provide a kind of safe space. You have to put things in the way of the person 'standing' so they can 'fall over' and thereby reveal themselves. You have to empathize but also challenge and provoke. Ask the awkward questions and even take the risk of infuriating them. You have to heckle … and most comics love to respond immediately when you do that and sometimes that finds its way into the show. So, I guess you are part audience, part heckler, part psychotherapist, part abuser. And sometime part architect and part wrecking ball. And – perhaps most importantly – you have to be no one. Just a kind of neutral point who creates obstacles to provoke creative ways of getting over them. The audience most definitely don't want to know anything about you, the director, in any shape or form. They want to see *themselves* as they watch, listen and laugh at the person behind the microphone. Or on the floor.

# 13

## Case study:

## *The Naked Racist*

Shows becoming more theatrical and ambitious, especially at the Edinburgh Fringe, has been a major factor in the growth of stand-up directing. Geoff Whiting observed first-hand Edinburgh stand-up directing beginning in the 2000s: 'I've been going to Edinburgh since '97, and that year I'm certain that if people were directing stand-up shows, it was very rare. But by 2003, 2004, you had people saying they had a director. And it became much more prevalent after Phil Nichol won the Perrier Award in 2006.' This was for *The Naked Racist* – and technically that year it was the 'if.comedy awards' but their sponsorship only lasted one year and people were still (happily for them) calling it by the name of the original sponsor.

In this chapter, we will take that show, the *Naked Racist*,[1] as a case study and explore how it came about and developed. The chapter is primarily in Phil's own words with input from his director on the show Phil Whelans, and from his current director John Gordillo. It touches on all sorts of subjects relevant to anyone aiming to do a full-length true-story festival show who wants to make a point (and this category covers *a lot* of Edinburgh shows).

Phil Nichol is an actor, stand-up, musician and director. He gigs on the comedy circuit and has performed full-length solo shows as a comic at the Edinburgh Fringe since 1996. He works with directors on his shows, and directs others. For Phil, 'Directors come in different shapes and sizes. The ones I like stay in the background.

They help you discover things and you don't even realize they are guiding you. I don't like a boss, I like a mentor.'

As a performer and a director, Phil Nichol has been a central figure in the development of this kind of emotionally ambitious show. He has come to specialize in storytelling shows with musical elements: 'I've always been a fan of the one-man theatre show. I saw a theatre piece by [stand-up and actor] Owen O'Neill [1997's *Off my Face*]: He did shows that were semi-autobiographical. I only say "semi-autobiographical" because he told me that he used theatrical devices and added other bits to the story to make them work. I remember watching the O'Neill show with Boothby Graffoe. At the end of it when the lights came on we were both in tears, as was most of the audience.'

Seeing his work made Phil Nichol think that stand-up could be equally ambitious in scope and emotion. And this kind of theatrical ambition leads naturally to the performer wanting a director. He subsequently did a trilogy of shows directed by Phil Whelans: *Nearly Gay* in 2005, *The Naked Racist* in 2006 and *Hiro Worship* in 2007.

> Owen O'Neal's advice to me was, 'Don't be afraid to be sincere and serious.' And Dave Gorman's advice to me was, 'Any jokes that you've got, that you put in because you need laughs, you want to take out as they remove the audience from the story, and then it makes the piece less effective because they stop believing.' They go, 'I know that bit is not true, because a minute before you've told a joke.' You have to use a lie to get to the joke. The laughs have to be honest laughs based on something. When I work with comedians I question them a lot on whether or not they're telling the truth.

If your material relies on the audience accepting that it's fundamentally true, any blatant untruth to get a laugh is at risk of jeopardizing their trust. Realist and sketch comics often make the assertion: *I swear this is true.* This is because a story that is recognized as true is often funnier than one the audience thinks is made up. I have actually worked with comics who were telling a story that came across as fabricated but was in fact true. Dialling down the exaggeration, putting in more detail and sacrificing some jokes all (paradoxically) help to increase the audience's laughter.

However, done sparingly, I feel you can have your cake and eat it if you make the joke and immediately acknowledge it's not true. An example is found in Dave Chappelle's 2017 special *The Age of Spin*, when he relates his first meeting with O. J. Simpson. He describes how Simpson's 'soon to be slain' wife embraced him affectionately. Chappelle recalls that as she held him 'for a long time' he whispered into her ear, 'Bitch, are you trying to get us both killed?' The audience explodes in laughter and as it subsides he adds, 'I'm just kidding. I didn't say that.'

A variation of this is to say what you really did say – and then add what you wished you'd said. For instance, Maria Bamford in her more personal 2017 special *Old Baby* relating how when she was told by a boyfriend that his father was in the mafia, said, 'Whoa, whoa, whoa!' She adds, 'What I could have [nonchalantly] said was, "I work in the entertainment industry. I am awash in filthy money! ... I'm paid in cash most nights with a gun on the table."' The reverse of this is to assert that you said something brilliant, or witty or extreme – and then withdraw it, revealing the feeble truth of what you actually said. The point of all this is so that the audience are clear when you're presenting something as true and when you are not. (Going into an idea that is hypothetical or speculative, and clearly making it as such, achieves the same end.)

As a stand-up performer, Phil Nichol is a *sensualist rebel sage,* if I might be permitted three archetypes. *The Naked Racist* is realist and anchored in truth but this reality is often suddenly amplified and played out as a grotesque cartoon. The show certainly operates on all of the levels I identify in Chapter 2 – the base level: sex, scatology and the body; emotional level: interpersonal dynamics and relationships; desire level: hungers, yearnings and egos; heart level: personal disclosures and revelations; mind level: language, analysis and opinions; philosophical level: ideas, theories and thoughts – and a case can be made for it touching the transcendent level too. Any show that is reaching all of these levels is a rich proposition.

*The Naked Racist* is an anti-war story of a drug-fuelled trip to Amsterdam. Phil told me, 'I wasn't thinking that I was in the running for any awards, because I'm at The Stand [a stand-up venue] in a tiny little room. All I was doing was trying to tell the story as best I could and I wanted the audience to understand that I thought that Tony Blair had taken us into an illegal war and that we needed to do something about it to stop it from happening again.' Phil always looks for the epiphany in shows he performs and directs. He gives the example of Jason Cook's 2007 Edinburgh show *Confessions*:

That was about: *call your dad*. That's what he boiled it down to. Very, very emotive concept. He probably took a lot of work to get it down to that. The question is: 'What is the epiphany?' It focusses the work. You work towards that epiphany. I use the term *epiphany* in the classical sense. It's the moment of realization for the performer in the story and it should be the same moment of realization for the audience. The epiphany that you have is personal. It's not preachy if you tell the story in a way that your character is able to re-live the moment where they had that epiphany. Then I believe the light will go on for the audience at the same time.'

The story of *The Naked Racist* culminates with Phil being chased naked through night-time Amsterdam by neo-Nazis and he ends up inadvertently becoming racist himself. He says the epiphany was, 'If you fight something with full force, you're going to become the thing you're fighting; you could become those fascists, if you continue to fight it in this way. I still believe that. If you *smash* the patriarchy, you worry me, because you've just become a volatile matriarchy. You're becoming the same people.' Phil described the origins of the show in his ill-fated solo trip to Amsterdam:

When it was happening, as I was being chased down the street naked by racists, I was not thinking, 'Oh, this is going to be my Edinburgh show!' Not in the slightest. I was actually going to do a different show. Then I did a stand-up gig at a night called *Four Kiwis Walk into a Bar* run by Terry Frisby, Jarred Christmas and Rhys Darby. I told them the story before I went on, and they laughed. I got an encore doing my normal comedy slot. I went back out and said, 'I'm wrecked. I've been up all night, I just came from Amsterdam.' Jarred and the others were going, 'Tell them the story.' I'm like, 'No, no, it's not funny, it's a story you tell your mates.' [In the end Phil relented.] So, I told the story but I rambled, I missed bits, and the audience is going, 'Sounds like just a drunken night in Amsterdam.'

This returns us to the point that stories we tell socially need work to become stand-up. In the case of the drunken Amsterdam story in the comedy club, Phil then did something you'd be unlikely to do socially. 'In the story I was naked and so to illustrate the point, then and there on a whim, I took my clothes off and put my shoes back on, to show the audience what it looked like. The reaction it got; they went bananas. People were coughing and snorting with laughter, and I thought, "This is something."'

Phil had been intending to do an anti-war show and had long been fascinated by the Doukhobors. He explained, 'They're the Russian immigrants to Canada. I was a bit obsessed with them and researched them. They're kind of long-haired orthodox Christians.' In *The Naked Racist,* Phil tells the story in the show of the Russians trying to force them to fight the Armenians and them refusing to compromise their pacifism and stripping naked to make their point. 'It kind of struck me as being a funny way of dealing with violence.' Suddenly the nudity of the Doukhobors and his own nudity in Amsterdam where he's facing down neo-Nazis became connected: 'It all came to me in a moment.' And other aspects of the story were suddenly resonant with the theme:

> I was talking to a guy earlier that night [in Amsterdam] who was this old American soldier. He'd become a mercenary bodyguard and boasted of his killings in Iraq. So that's crazy. I started to realize that if I told the story right, it could be a reaction to the illegal invasion of Iraq, which was what I was working on anyway. Then I realized the whole story started because of a conflict [a row with his girlfriend, who then refused to come]. So, I was there accidentally by myself because of a little tiny thing. It genuinely happened because of a joke about her bunions. I made a bad joke. It wasn't till I started putting the show together with Phil [Whelans], the director, that we were able to see the threads and go, 'Well, I was going to write a show about this subject anyway and now I've got the story that actually illustrates it.'

Director Phil Whelans recalled:

> As a kid I went to see Spalding Grey's autobiographical monologues, and Ken Campbell as well – shows like *Recollections of a Furtive Nudist*. They were like one-man shows with a storytelling element, led by a charismatic, compelling performer. That was in my mind with Phil's show: It's like a one-man show,

but it still has all the energy of stand-up. I wanted it to be stand-up, but with far more ambition. It's full-fat stand-up. He sings songs, a band comes out and by the end he's got no clothes on. It helped that it was on at The Stand where everyone expected it to be just a man or a woman talking into a microphone for fifty minutes.

From small beginnings this climactic nudity became epic. Phil Nichol recalls:

The first few nights [in the original Edinburgh run], I was just getting naked by myself. It was shocking and fun and the audience would go, 'Ooh, it's a very small room.' I'm not a natural exhibitionist, so I was becoming comfortable with it. Then I had the idea of getting a few other people naked so I got my sound guy to do it. And I had a band in the show. They're friends of mine. I had brought them up to Edinburgh to play and then two days into the show I realized, 'If the idea is we're doing a spoof of 1960's flower-power, anti-Vietnam culture, then you guys have to be naked as well.' So, they did it. Then Janice, my girlfriend at the time, she was like, 'That looks like fun.' Then I told [sketch group] Pappy's what we were doing and they went, 'We'll do it.' Then Phil Kay showed up. He's an exhibitionist, anyway. I put him in the front row, and every night he got up pretending to be a member of the audience. I thought, 'If I could actually get the audience naked, that'd be amazing', and that's where that idea was born. It would be a spoof of the counter culture and also, with me telling the audience that I thought Tony Blair had taken us into an illegal war, it would actually *be* the thing that it's spoofing. By the end of the Edinburgh run I had twenty nude people a night. The room only holds fifty people! All while the band sang a song called *Get the Troops Out*.

I saw *The Naked Racist* after Edinburgh as part of the Edinburgh Comedy Award shows at The Garrick, a lovely old West End theatre in London, where the nudity seemed to have an extra level of anarchy and subversion. Phil recalled:

I thought it worked really well there, because we were able to have stooges all the way through the audience. The audience were not a festival audience and so were more reserved, certainly not expecting to go out that night and get naked. But I do remember members of the audience getting into it. I'd worked up a speech in order to make it happen. I had about forty or so naked people on stage in the end. I did it the next year in Edinburgh at the [Pleasance] Grand and I had one-hundred-and-eleven naked people. It was not sexual. It became easier and easier to get people to do it, as they realized that you're just being human, natural and naked, which is probably what was happening in the counter-culture.

All of this came out of a true story that initially Phil didn't even think was a show and yet in the end it actually had some really big ideas in it, but it wasn't forced. It emerged. John Gordillo observed:

You have to be careful. Once [the agenda] gets in the story, it can become didactic and boring. I think actually in my own work [as a stand-up] I've fallen a bit foul of that. I've been very driven by certain issues. There's no journey there if you say 'This is the thing!' There has to be some discovery. That's where I feel it can be a problem with being too didactic, and when you try and make everything fit the scheme. Because then you've come up with your conclusion before you've written it. [Stanley] Kubrick said, 'The easiest thing in the world is knowing what your story is about. But the hardest thing is covering it up.' I think that is a very, very true comment about art and storytelling. Can something work that has an agenda? I mean Mark Thomas can do it, a few people can. But I think that art and stories are not political tracts. What's beautiful is they can deal with massive issues but in the form of metaphor. I've got another Kubric quote. Sorry, he's very quotable: 'If you try and write about the world. You'll end up with nothing. But if you try and write about one thing, you end up with the world.' One of the notes that I always give to people is be specific. If I get riled up about this vape pen, how annoying it is when the battery runs out, or whatever my issues with it are, as long as I commit to exploring my issues with the vape pen you don't have to be a vaper to understand the role that plays in my life. We all have those things in our lives. People don't have to have done exactly what you've done in order to project into you and to identify with you. The more *little* you make it, in a way the bigger the picture.

# 14

# Stand-ups do theatre

With stand-ups doing increasingly theatrical shows, the next logical step is to actually do theatre. A stand-up who also stretched the comedy form and ultimately jumped ship to entirely theatrical shows is Mark Thomas, a *crusader jester*. Having pushed stand-up into a more interactive, storytelling dimension, in the end, the stories and issues he wanted to address were not best served by the quick, laugh-driven format of a stand-up set. He told me: 'I don't do stand-up any more. I tell people if you want to see a stand-up show there are lots of good new folk about go and see them. In fact, if you watch Dave more than three times a week don't come to the show. I am working on the next three shows, and only one of them comes vaguely near stand-up and even then I wouldn't bet on it.' Nevertheless, Mark, of course, brings into his theatre shows all of the skills he has developed in stand-up: being in the present moment, working the room, pacing, timing, delivering a natural conversational performance that punches out key ideas. And the shows are funny, just not so relentlessly having to be focused on the laughs. I asked him when his stand-up work started to become closer to storytelling and theatre:

> The stuff I do has been heading this way since the nineties. I loved running campaigns against Post Office privatisation from the stage, and inevitably these turned into stories. What I do is very simple: I go and do things, I create a story, and then I come and tell it. Even when I was doing telly, I was urging the producer to let me do a show which was just me telling stories and no footage being played into the show. But I suppose the first big story was the Ilisu Dam Campaign – I was a campaign

founder – which was about fighting a dam-building scheme in the Kurdish region of Turkey. I remember doing an interview with a journalist in Scotland who was flabbergasted that I would do a two-hour show about fighting a dam in Kurdistan. But it worked and ever since then the shows have been primarily about telling stories. Officially, the first theatrical show was *Bravo Figaro*, which was about my dad and opera and a condition he had called Progressive Supranuclear Palsy. I had talked about my dad on Radio 4 and by complete chance, some people from the Royal Opera House heard the broadcast and asked if I would meet the film director Mike Figgis, who was the curator of the ROH festival that year. We met, and he commissioned me to do a show. The result was the start of *Bravo Figaro*.

When we spoke, Mark was touring his show *The Red Shed* that celebrates the fiftieth birthday of the titular Red Shed in Wakefield, a wooden hut that doubles up as a Labour Club and thirty years ago was the venue for Mark's first stand-up gigs. In the show, he tells the story of his political coming of age along with the tales of the people who inspired him. Mark also brings volunteers on stage to take on the roles of various characters in the story. He explains: '*The Red Shed* is all about community and collective memory, so I wanted people to come and see a show that couldn't work unless the audience joins in and creates a sense of community. So, I very nicely ask people to help me on stage, each night they add a little bit of chaos and improvisation which is huge fun. To be honest, the volunteers each bring something different, but the jobs they are asked to do are set into the script. The way they do it is the chaos. And very nice and beautiful it is too.' I wondered how the real people from the stories he tells have reacted to the show. Mark responded, 'Generally well. An artist who is mentioned in the show has been to see it four times. My favourite reaction was from a man called Richard who saw the show and said, "Someone came up to me and said, 'Did you really say that?' I said, 'Yes I did. But I said it in the sub-committee not the committee.'"' Through the production Mark hopes 'to create a show people have not seen before, to be original in the telling of working-class stories and their importance.' Joe Douglas directed *The Red Shed*. I asked Mark what a director brings to his work: 'I am very lucky to work with him. I have had a number of directors and what they do is make me look at all the different ways I can to tell a story and question the integrity of the work and the story, to make me constantly re-examine the work to make sure it's true.'

Daniel Kitson is a stand-up who straddles comedy, storytelling and theatre shows. In a (rare) interview, in *The Skinny* from 2007, he discusses the differences he finds between writing stand-up and storytelling shows: 'With stand-up, I have an idea or a feeling and I talk around it and into it. Stories very much have to be written out and learnt. Phrasing and pace and so on are massively key because I want it to resonate beyond the moment.' When he first did a story show, *A Made Up Story*, he was concerned about the reactions of the stand-up audience. 'It was the first story show I did – in 2003. That one really split people: people loved it, people hated it, and worst of all, people admired the intention but thought it wasn't very good. That plays into your fears about your work in a fairly accurate and saddening way. But by the time *Stories for the Wobbly Hearted* came around in 2005 there was a watershed moment when I realised I just had to commit to the thing from the start, no pre-emptive apology or warning or explanation. Just commit to the nature of the thing.'

In one way though, these storytelling shows are more akin to stand-up than a theatrical monologue: 'I've been asked if I would license the text for others to perform and I wouldn't do that. It's entirely personal – it's mine, it's me telling my story. There would be something fundamentally wrong with someone else speaking it. It's not a play. It's me talking.'[1] And having seen a *play* for two performers by Daniel Kitson, *Tree* at the Old Vic in London in 2015, I feel even here, in a play text, that Kitson's character (who he plays) is very much speaking with his own voice. It's hard to imagine any other actor doing it.

Maggie Inchley has cast stand-ups in productions of classic plays including *The School for Scandal*, *The Zoo Story* and *Talk Radio*. She explained to me: 'I worked for quite a long time doing The Comedians Theatre Company and took shows up to Edinburgh. I worked a lot with [co-founder] Phil Nichol.' Maggie discussed the categories in the Fringe brochure, where these shows were listed under 'theatre': 'I think it's a false boundary and it causes a lot of problems. We try to resist it but every time you go to Edinburgh you have to put it in a section of the programme. So, you say "This is comedy" or "This is theatre." It winds you up because so much theatre is funny and so much comedy is theatrical. It feels false to me and a real instrument of marketing rather than something that serves what you're creating.' I asked her what the differences were between directing actors in a play and comedians:

> First of all, it's not a correct assumption to say 'comedian or actor' because a lot of them do both. Some comedians I've worked with have had proper actor training. Others haven't had any at all. They haven't got any idea about blocking or the technical aspects of staging, and often they take their references from films rather than from the stage. Some of them actively dislike theatre! But assuming we're talking about a comedian with no acting training, from a director's point of view, the difference between working with comedians and actors is often to do with discipline and spontaneity. Without the acting training, I think you're going to get more of a sense of spontaneity but that sometimes makes it hard for the director because the performer is probably going to do something different every day. From the audience's point of view, however, it can be very exciting to watch that, and you often get a sense of authenticity.

Theatre director Mike Alfreds champions this freedom for actors to create afresh every night, setting out his ideas in the book *Different Every Night*. Maggie recognizes this: 'I think you can get a really nice sense of that with skilful comedians if they're in tune with each other.'

Stand-ups of course continually revise and rewrite material in light of audience reactions and Maggie has experienced comics wanting to do that with plays: 'With stand-ups there is a tendency to want to edit and change the material. They're used to working on their own material, and a lot of it is very rhythmic and technical. If stand-ups spot anything in a script they don't think will work, they will often want to rewrite. As a director, if you agree with a stand-up's suggestion, it means you have to do some negotiating with the writer – and some writers are more into that than others.' Another challenge is logistical: 'One of the practical difficulties of doing a play with comics in Edinburgh, is you've got a competition for the comedian's time. They'll be doing their own show too, so you're unlikely to get what you'd get with an actor; which is very often, complete dedication and discipline towards this one thing that they're realizing. To the extent where some will stay in character. But in my experience, you are unlikely to get that with most comedians. Having said that, I do think Phil Nichol is a phenomenal actor, and he has had acting training too.' Maggie identifies comedy that straddles the two worlds: 'With Alan Francis, he does storytelling and he's actually an actor as well. He will do these long stories that he does rehearse and sculpt very carefully, like a piece of theatre, but then the way he will perform is to just leave enough room on the night to make it sound spontaneous, so it doesn't come out in exactly the same words every night. I think there is a blend going on there. A hybrid form which is neither stand-up nor theatre but a bit of both.'

I asked Simon McBurney about directing Lenny Henry in his stand-up show, *So Much Things to Say* (2003) that went into fresh areas for the comic and how, ultimately, he went on to do theatre. He told me:

I felt that I could help by confronting him with questions that perhaps others had never put to him. Both in performance and in content. In performative terms, we worked on setting up elements that would ultimately come together – or rather reveal themselves – in a final section; in which all the people and ideas of the show would collide and revolve simultaneously as a climax to the show. That was a kind of tour de force of juggling dozens of verbal, physical, and cerebral … bits … that would collide and explode like a firework display of revelation and hilarity. I am not sure we absolutely succeeded at first, but that was not the point. The point was that the difficulty of trying to achieve this aim, the rest of the show revealed itself to us. Both its form and content. And perhaps it was a signal to Lenny that he was also really interested in moving towards the theatre. The content of *So Much Things to Say* was revelatory. And was transitional into the kind of work he makes today. And I guess my job was to push him. Cut bits off him. Ask him difficult questions … in fact he just reminded me, in a video, that he sent me for my birthday, that I'm the only person who can make him cry in rehearsal. I am not sure that was true … it could be apocryphal! *So Much Things to Say* became a transitional piece. Lenny talked about his upbringing. In Dudley. About immigration. What it means to leave one place. And arrive somewhere else. That once that journey is made, there is no 'going back'. What do you bring with you? The violence of leaving behind. The violence you encounter on arrival. Doesn't sound that funny. And Lenny would walk round the room saying, 'but it's got to be funny, it has to be funny. Where are the gags?'. Sometimes looking for the familiar thing as a support. I always played devil's advocate by saying: don't worry about being funny. You are funny. Something will occur. 'Yeah, but where are the jokes? Simon, I need jokes.' It was a piece that addressed his own experiences but he knew it would be delivered to a dominantly white audience, until he got to the Hackney Empire. He dug very deep. And I tried to provide a few words of encouragement and ideas about where to excavate as he built the foundations for another phase of his artistic life. It was a humbling experience to watch his unwavering determination and his unflinching courage as he peeled off his clothes and revealed layers within.

# 15

# Theatre makers influenced by stand-up

Having explored stand-ups moving into the world of theatre, in this chapter we look at the reverse journey: theatre makers entering into, and being influenced by, the world of stand-up. Hannah Ringham is a theatre maker and co-founder of the experimental company Shunt. I worked with Hannah when she wanted to explore stand-up to feed into her one-woman show *I Want Love* (2017, Hackney Town Hall, Birmingham Repertory Theatre). She said, 'I thought I would try to understand the form better and take the bits from the show that I thought were particularly *stand-up* into a comedy context.' So, we took material from the theatrical monologue, reworked it as stand-up and she then performed it.

The immediacy, simplicity and directness of stand-up interests Hannah: 'You stand up in front of the audience and you speak and [from the audience] it's a "Yes" or "No" immediately. And if the audience doesn't respond, the stand-up says [in effect], "Are you there?" That seems a fundamental thing. In all the stand-ups that I've watched, there is a general understanding that the comic, if they're not getting a response, they will interrogate that.' Hannah's initial stand-up performance was at the new act night at *Downstairs at the Kings Head* in Crouch End in London.

With an audience who have come to see a stand-up show, there is a sort of looseness; people are more relaxed, they're more up for stuff. Crudely, with a theatre audience, maybe they're not so relaxed. In a comedy gig, there is a different expectation in the air. The idea of *entertainment* is more present, the idea that this is *live* and it's going to be funny *now*. In theatre, the expectation might be more to do with a long investment in narrative. And the set-up is so incredibly simple. You don't need anything. You just stand up. And you have a series of different people with different points of view where you hear the audience go: 'funny', 'not interested', 'bored', 'I love this', 'I hate this'. And they're maybe homophobic, sexist, racist, all of those things, and the audience might tell them they are. So, it feels very live to me. Sometimes I think in the theatre, things get in the way. With Shakespeare, with the Globe, it was a very live thing where people would turn up and they would shout at the stage, 'It's a boy' when someone comes on and they're dressed as a woman but they're obviously a man. [Now] the theatre has become very formal regarding what is accepted as the protocol. Which doesn't mean to say that I think stand-up is better. I just see that live element as really exciting; for the theatre to learn from, or for me to learn from.

I asked Hannah how the feeling of performing stand-up differed from a theatrical performance:

There's less of a barrier between you and the audience – it feels inherently closer. In stand-up, I feel the immediacy of the response from the audience in a way that is different from theatre. The response in the theatre can be more ethereal. In comedy, it's quick responses. I really felt the direct engagement when people were with me and I really felt it when they slipped away. Sometimes it's harder to tell in theatre! Allowing for the reaction of the audience is an important part of it – which I know from theatre, but at the same time there is a different pace. It's quicker.

Another difference from conventional theatre was as Hannah put it, 'playing the space literally'. At the outset, we had her say: 'So, I'm here in Crouch End'. Hannah observes, 'If I had said "So, I'm here in the Bahamas," people would imagine the Bahamas *and* they know they are in a pub. We do not suppose anything else.' The audience doesn't suspend their disbelief and agree they are in the Bahamas. It's both the pub and an idea of the Bahamas:

This is a very exciting simple thought for me. It has immediate roots in Brechtian theatre; understanding the world you are in and imagining another world at the same time. I suppose comedy is always about juxtaposition. In the theatre, there is often a set, so the question of where we are might start from is a more complex point. [At the King's Head new act night] I saw this lovely woman, she was great, come on and say 'I'm a bat.' And that was really funny. It was very literal. She's *not* and she says she *is*. So, we find it funny. In stand-up, we know she is *not* a bat. But in theatre it can become 'the great question of the bat. Am I a bat, or not a bat?'

Hannah's theatrical monologue was already in a conversational idiom, so that fit with the stand-up context. Then extracting material from it to make a stand-up set meant first identifying the comic ideas, which in the original text were sometimes subtle or ambiguous. One of the main changes was around ambiguity. In stand-up, ambiguity very much has a place *in the set-up*. This is misdirection. Then when you get to the *payoff* everyone needs to be on the same page. Your point needs to be clear. Theatre has a much higher tolerance of, or even a demand for, the meaning remaining open to interpretation *throughout*. Hannah found this new way of looking at her material to be 'a bit of a head-fuck, but actually in a good way, because I started to clearly see the contrast of objectives between doing stand-up and doing a theatre piece. In stand-up: *Set-up – ambiguity/payoff – not*. In theatre things can be left unresolved.'

When we were looking through the material, finding stuff to put in front of a stand-up audience, I had a strong sense of needing to get to the idea quicker. We've got to set it up and then reveal the comic idea. Then the audience react: Is it funny or not? And then we've got to set up the next thing. That seemed to be doing something different from how the ideas are presented in theatre. Hannah agreed: 'I think speed is a big thought. With stand-up, it's just quicker. That's what I love and question about it. A quick response feels like a great thing *and* at times not so great. I have heard amazing stand-up comedians who take you somewhere deeply philosophical, but I think there can be a tendency in the form that doesn't allow for questions that aren't necessarily funny straight away.'

Hannah recalled an example of a theatre show that emphatically was not aiming to please straight away: 'I remember going to see a show about ten years ago that affected me a lot. It was *The Show*

*Must Go On* by the choreographer Jerome Bel. It started off with
an incredibly slow fade out of the stage lights over ten minutes.
Nobody was on stage.' There was nothing to do except watch this
almost imperceptible fading of the lights:

> And I sat there in the audience thinking, 'This is shit. There's
> nothing happening. Is this a joke? Are they taking the piss out of
> me?' Then I'd think, 'This is exciting, I haven't seen this before.'
> Then, 'This is shit. Shall I go?' And on and on. Until finally, after
> ten minutes, which is an incredibly long time on stage, the lights
> went out into darkness. And then the lights came up and there
> were thirty people on stage and then they started dancing. I loved
> it because I had gone through the process of thinking, 'Do I give
> a shit? Don't I give a shit?' I was struggling. My struggle as an
> audience member was interesting. With stand-up, *no matter
> what*, the comedian is always saying, 'Are you there, audience?'
> That feels like a through line with every comedian. Yes, they can
> build an hour show, or two hours or more, and that can be a
> show with complex structure but there is this understanding: If
> the audience isn't with you, it's over. With theatre that's not the
> case. You can do a piece of theatre and the audience might not
> be with you and that's what you're exploring.

When I did my Theatre Studies and English degree, I remember
first seeing a short Samuel Beckett piece and feeling it was unlike
anything I'd ever seen. A fellow student remarked: 'My god that
was tedious.' And it was. It alienated the audience. And yet it so
clearly wasn't trying to be entertaining that I suddenly felt that the
audience feeling bored and alienated must be part of the point. And
then, going on to discover works like *Waiting for Godot*, I found
the comedy in Beckett's pieces and the playfulness with the live
situation too. Hannah commented:

> The thing about Beckett is there is an existential idea of being
> with the audience. I went to see this Beckett piece at the Old
> Vic, performed by this really good actor. [*A selection of Samuel
> Beckett's Texts For Nothing*, performed by Lisa Dwan, 2016.]
> There was a lot of clapping, almost the kind of hero worship you
> get with comedians. And at one point this actor – who is on her
> own on the stage, which is part of the parallel for me – she says

'What do I do when silence falls?' Now, the way she said it, made it about her experiencing silence falling *on her*. Now, theatre can be about that – the audience *watching* someone experience something. However, for me she missed a trick, or the director did. While Beckett is playing with the ideas of life and death, there is still that deep connection with the audience and it's all about being present and direct. So, when she says that line, we as a collective audience, understand it's about the theatre. She's saying it in a theatre. She says it alone, but *we're there* – and the biggest joke is we're not going to say anything. Silence falls. For me, it's about the live experience of us all in the room together. I think sometimes the theatre, as we understand it today, doesn't allow itself that visceral live experience that is so present in stand-up. Because people are so concerned about the idea of watching something that doesn't include the audience. That's a fundamental thing. It's got to be a conversation, otherwise make a film. Even if you spend the whole show talking to the other actor, we still need to know it's a conversation.

Hannah reflected on her stand-up performances, 'I strongly felt the basic question of: "Is it funny?" When I did stand-up, sometimes it was and sometimes it wasn't. And I watched people perform and sometimes they were and sometimes they weren't. It's scary when it's not funny. But it can also be interesting. You use the word "release." [As in "tension/release."] And that's an interesting thought. Especially now, because fuck we all need a release. And then what is beyond that?'

## Stand-up influence in theatre

Having taken material from Hannah Ringham's monologue and put it into a stand-up context, the next part of the work was for me to see a dress rehearsal of the theatre show and to feed back on it from a stand-up perspective. Hannah said of her work with Shunt, 'We weren't into traditional spaces and we didn't do traditional work. We played a lot with audience interaction. So, I've always been interested in a direct relationship with the audience. You *can* have that in theatre, but you don't always. Hopefully, you're always paying attention to them but you're not necessarily having a direct interaction with them.' It was this direct communication that a stand-up has with an audience that interested Hannah about the form.

She went on, 'With my new show, I'm interested in the idea of different forms meeting each other and how they interact and interrogating that. I've always been interested in comedy and with *I Want Love*, elements of my writing for the piece felt quite stand-up.' In *I Want Love*, Hannah is in character but she's directly talking to the audience. At one point, she's talking about the building that we're in. I said, 'Well, we're in Hackney Town Hall. Name it.' So suddenly she is in character, doing a fictional monologue, but she's talking about the precise building where she's performing. There was another moment in the show where she says, 'I could just walk out that door', and she indicates the door to the space. This line was underplayed, and I felt it could be more explicit: Make them realise it literally is the door to this theatre and you're saying, 'I could just stop this show right now and I could just leave, and you'd all be left sitting here.' Hannah recalled: 'What was refreshing about a comedy director's perspective was the immediacy of the awareness.'

The show is about the character's attempts to get love. There was a moment in the middle of the show that acknowledged the audience, and the need to please them. I suggested she ramp that up a lot, and that it could become the ending of the show, which would bring it right into *this* moment: I need the love of *you*, the audience. Hannah made this change: 'It made sense to end with a question, which is so fundamental in all theatre or performance.' I discussed the show with John Gordillo, and he observed, 'And that is presumably, the highest stakes, the most vulnerable thing. The biggest thing she could do in that show would be to have done that. It leads you to that moment of exposure. That's what you want the most.' John Gordillo sees a commonality between theatrical and stand-up directing: 'I don't see directing stand-up, when you're making a show, as being any different to any other kind of directing. I think it's simply how can you tell a great story with the tools that you've got. So, you're still asking the same questions of the material with a stand-up as you would of the script of *12 Years a Slave*. It's just got to envelop you or compel you in some way. Sometimes those goals are a bit too lofty for a stand-up because you're not dealing with such a broad emotional palette. But regarding the basic storytelling principles: exactly the same.' When we spoke, John was directing a theatre piece performed by a woman and her father. It was based on their real relationship and history together. He said: 'I realised this isn't going to work if the two of them are *acting* out the situations and we [the audience] know they've done this fifty times already. I said, "I think this is going to be better if you just *tell us*." In that sense, it's bringing stand-up presentation. [The father will say] "This is what happened next" and then he tells us. Then: "This is what happened after that." Then any disagreement between them is almost like a therapy session. [And not a re-enactment.] It means you don't have to act. It's trying to work out what method will be the most authentic and be immediate for, again, the people and the tools that you have at your disposal. Yes, it's always the same, but immediacy is always the goal anyway, isn't it? Whatever form you're working in.' Here we see primacy given to direct communication in the moment rather than a passive witnessing on the part of the audience. Hannah commented:

> I think you see that [stand-up influence] in quite a lot of theatre these days. I've seen a lot of performances where people begin with talking to the audience and then it goes off into other areas. For example, I saw Robert Lepage recently. [In this solo show *887* at the Barbican in July 2017.] And he began by telling a personal story. It was just him talking to the audience, sharing something personal, which feels very stand-up. He had been asked to do a poem for a recital, but he couldn't memorize it. The whole show became about memory, who he was, where he came from and his struggle with the content of the poem.

Naming a problem that you the performer are struggling with and then making that the content is a standard stand-up approach. Hannah suggested a (bathetic set-up/payoff) stand-up example: 'Greg Davies coming on and saying, "Let me tell you where I'm at. My underpants' elastic just broke."' That's a problem that is very present and on his mind. She went on: 'And with Tim Crouch, [in his shows] because he sets it up that he can talk to, and relate truthfully to, the audience, he can say things like "I forgot the script. I've forgotten the words right now." A part of *who he is*, is in the story. But if he came on in a pair of tights just doing the whole classical situation he could never do that.'

In *887*, Lepage also talked to the audience about the set he had on stage; referring to the immediate environment is a classically stand-up thing to do. And, in an echo of Phil Nichol's *The Weary Land,* at the end of *887* Lepage at last spoke the poem. Hannah recalled that, 'He totally went for it! But what made it grounded, was this whole hour and a half that led up to it, exploring ideas, chatting about his life and asking, "Who am I to say this? Who are we [the audience] in this?" Then, in the end, for him to go for it with all his heart and soul was an interesting contrast to the way that he'd been talking, exploring and thinking. And that's very powerful.'

Simon McBurney also explored memory in his piece *Mnemonic* (2003) and it too began with direct address to the audience. He told me:

> When I made *Mnemonic*, a quite serious piece about memory, it essentially started with a piece of stand-up. I just came out with the microphone and spoke to the audience. And yes, it had at its core the soil of personal experience. I had broken up a long-term relationship and that formed the central spine of the story. And we all, all the performers, drew on deeply personal experiences to feed this piece we were making.

Hannah continued: 'I think there's freedom to play with the present moment in the form of stand-up, which is sometimes negated in theatre. You go and see something traditional and ask "Is this a living, present moment? Is this existing now or is this about something that existed before and does not take in the live-ness of the total event, the audience, the whole live experience?"' Often in theatre, they're trying to *do it* in the way that they've done it before: in the way that they did it in rehearsal or the way they did it last night. Hannah describes the attitude of actors in a conventional theatre piece: 'We're trying not to be influenced by anything extraneous.' Whereas with stand-up the extraneous can be part of the content. Oliver Double talked about this in a stand-up education context: 'I had this phrase, "It's all sandwiches." I was talking about how if you're taking a physical theatre course for example, quite rightly, the tutor will probably insist on you not talking about what you've been doing outside the class; what sandwiches you've just had. But with stand-up, *it's all sandwiches*. It's all things from outside the class. It's not about stripping things back to nothing; it's about what you bring with you.'

At the time of writing, I am directing Stroud-based writer/actor Helen Wood in a new Edinburgh show about Ordnance Survey maps and every time she tells me of some comic difficulty she has had in the research and development of the show I say, 'Put that in.' For example, in the show she takes the audience on a 'virtual walk' around part of the Cotswolds and I told her to actually go and walk it and take photos to use in the show. At one point, she was trying to get a photo in a tourist information centre and the woman serving refused to be in the picture – but the man agreed and furthermore said he wanted to be photographed in front of the tea towels. Helen was just telling *me* this, but of course it had to go in the show.

I told Dec Munro the topic of the show and he remarked, 'I love when a performer is passionate about something that other people haven't really talked about. If your obsession is with Jilly Cooper or with stamp collecting, that's great. Because if you're going to do it eighty times and you're going to tour all over the world, you want to care, and when you're being interviewed for the one-hundred-and-fiftieth time about Ordnance Survey maps, you really want to be in a position where that actually matters to you.' Helen described her first steps in stand-up: 'I spent years in community theatre. Back then, I was always in character. So, when I did my first stand-up weekend course I automatically took on a character because that's all I knew. Then when I did the first stand-up course with you, you said, "Stop playing a character and be authentic." That was very helpful.' When I directed what became her first one-woman show (*What Kind of Fool Am I?* Edinburgh Fringe 2016), she told me she wanted to do a comic show about the Enneagram personality system. She said, 'I'm going to portray characters that represent all the nine personality types.' I asked Helen why she wanted to talk about the Enneagram and when she told me her story of discovering the system and how much it had benefitted her, I said, '*That's* the show. Your personal story is the show.' Initially, the idea of being on stage and talking directly to the audience was quite a leap. Helen recalled, 'I'd thought it'd be the nine characters in a play. It never occurred to me to do anything else. Then I realized that I love going to see other people's shows that are autobiographical. I think it was a lack of confidence: "My life's not very interesting." But of course, when you think about it, everyone's life is interesting. In the end, people told me they could relate to my show because it *was* just me telling them about my life. I ended up having so many people saying, "Well, that's exactly my life."'

Now Helen has worked in a more stand-up way, she sees the limitations in one-woman shows that don't break the fourth wall. For example, she saw an autobiographical show 'where the writer/performer was just emerging from having had children, and she was just characters, she wasn't herself at all. I wasn't as engaged as I felt I would be. You were very much watching her *present* something, rather than engage us. She performed it very well, she was all full of energy, but there was something missing.' Helen, however, didn't want to relinquish playing characters entirely. So, we arrived at a hybrid format that is autobiographical stand-up in its presentation *and* she will then perform a character or characters from her life. This is done in a more theatrical way than an *act-out,* drawing in elements like props and music: 'I'm feeling I'm getting the best of both worlds. I feel more passionate about theatre than pure stand-up comedy. And I'm much more comfortable putting my shows into the theatre section of the [Edinburgh Fringe] programme [rather than comedy]. And I love playing around with different characters and accents.' And, as with Robert Lepage talking directly and honestly with the audience or the happy accident of Eleanor Conway doing some audience chat before going into her show proper, because the audience has met Helen *as herself* they are more on board with the theatrical content; they can see *Helen* enjoying doing a character. Whereas, in a show when Helen comes on from the beginning as a character, she has to hide her glee about playing a role.

I directed a new comic play, *In Tents and Purposes,* initially seen in 2016 at Lyric Theatre Hammersmith and the Vaults Festival in London and then at Assembly in the Edinburgh Fringe 2016. Written by Roxy Dunn and performed by Roxy and Alys Metcalf, it was an official sell-out at the Fringe, and in 2017 it had a national tour and two stints at Soho Theatre. The play explored fate, belief and free will through the story of two friends leaving university and the next ten years of their lives. As well as directing, I took a dramaturgical role and helped develop the text. In our first meeting, thinking with my stand-up hat on, I put it to Roxy that we might introduce a second layer to the show where she and Alys came out of character between scenes and spoke to the audience as themselves.

Roxy embraced the idea. She says now, 'I think everyone who saw the show agrees that it lifted the show to a whole other level.' Alys added, 'I think it's a nice way for the audience to feel like they know us. It was almost like them buying into us as people was a way to get them to buy into the play.' So, as well as finding the characterization of the fictional characters, we developed their on-stage personas. As with stand-up, we were wanting their personas to be authentic and drawing on their less attractive qualities. Alys recalls, 'Finding the most clownish, ridiculous parts of yourself was a simple way into finding the funny stuff. Our worst character traits and our insecurities are naturally funny to explore. I enjoyed it *and* it felt like a bit of a cheat because we know those parts of us so we can naturally play them.'

The show begins as a regular play, and it's only after the first scene that the actors break the fourth wall, speak to the audience as themselves and then the meta side is revealed. Roxy has a strong sense of the audience reaction at this moment: 'I feel like they go, "I thought I knew what my part was in this as an audience member and has that changed now?" You can feel them going, "Hang on, is this actually happening? And then, does that mean we're about to get involved in a way that we hadn't initially bought into?"' This is about the contract the performers have with the audience. In a conventional play, the audience's side of the bargain is that they agree to sit quietly and attentively. Here the show is playing with their expectations of their role. Hannah Ringham commented on this moment in the show: 'It's your responsibility [as an actor] to take care of that so that the audience can feel that the uncomfortable thing is interesting and funny.' Roxy was surprised that 'quite a few people who saw the show thought we were improvising the "meta" bits. I found that very interesting. I met with somebody the other week who said "It's all improvised" and I had to explain, "No, I actually wrote it." In that sense, it's not that far from stand-up where there's a common misconception that it's made up on the spot. I think they're impressed but they also potentially feel a bit cheated. It's sort of lying.' Alys added, 'Where it's different to stand-up was us not knowing quite how much we should be ad-libbing when the audience [feeling freed from their usual contract] occasionally started talking back. You're thinking, "We need to be careful because this isn't actually within the show."'

The metanarrative and the play became thoroughly entwined. For example, in one scene in the narrative of the *play*, the characters are at a wedding reception and Roxy's character is talking about hitting on a guy who's on the other side of the room. She rehearses her lines as if speaking to him, for Alys's character's feedback. In the performance, the two actors look out into the audience and pick a man – who they identify by what he's wearing – and treat that man as if *he* is across the room in the wedding, oblivious to what is going on. Invariably, the man would smile and squirm – and people around him would find his involvement funny. Hannah described how the audience here become implicated in the fiction of a play: 'The audience know that they have a presence in the room: "They [the actors] know that I'm here. They understand that I'm a part of this."'

Hannah feels that direct address to the audience is particularly welcome *now*: 'Stand-up starts saying everything directly to the audience and you immediately engage with them. I think people respond "Oh my God, thank you for talking to me directly." There's so much *in the way* around us, I just want to *meet* other people. People just want to go, "Hello. Are you all right? You're a human being; I'm a human being. We're human beings. This is the show."'

To draw the discussion to a close and to bring the subject back round to stand-up, I asked Simon McBurney about the persona – the comedic self – with which we started the book, and how this relates to direct address, the connection between the performer and the audience that we have latterly explored:

> With our particular moment in history where we have become increasingly self-obsessed, it seems to me there are two aspects that relate to that with stand-up comedy; one is the fact that each individual comic tends to ply their wares by exposing the self. I mean was there a self before Freud? Or have we invented this curious thing called the 'self'. Certainly, it is at the core of stand-up. Ripping into one's 'self'. And secondly, I believe there is something beautiful and also important about this: standing up and falling over in front of people. And by falling over of course I mean exposing oneself, failing, in every way, this keys into the human desire to connect. Connect because we see what we recognize and keep hidden. To see your own idiocy, which you thought was private, reflected straight back at you from the

stage – and in that moment realizing you are not alone. That what we think is ours and ours only, this individual 'self', is, perhaps, just another pretension of our times, a shared fiction. And for a moment, perhaps, when we see this, when we realize what is being exposed, we are taken away from this self-absorbed human identity where we end up just looking into screens, and realise we are all interconnected. I dunno if that is true! But I would love to think so.

# Afterword:

# The end

Dear reader (it seems apt to drop fully into direct address right at
the last), I am writing this, the end of the book, on the very day
it has to be submitted to the publisher. My problem is – I need
an ending. (I'm practising what I preach here, making the external
issue the content.) It's struck me that the only way to end the book
is to do it like a stand-up show. So, what were those ending types I
suggested again?

1  *The callback, where something from earlier is unexpectedly*
   *brought back*. Okay, I'm doing that one. This whole bit is a
   callback to Chapter 11.

2  *The false dawn – everything seems back to normal ... then*
   *it isn't*. Right, seriously. it is time to get back to normal. You
   can't end a book like this. ... Actually, yes you can. It's *my*
   book, and if you're reading this, it means this conceit got
   through the editor.

3  *A call-to-action – now do this*. Making the call to action
   'hire me as a director' would be too evidently self-serving.
   And inviting you to apply ideas from this book in your
   own stand-up work would be too obvious. I guess, instead,
   my call to action is for you, in whatever way you can, to
   acknowledge, appreciate and discuss the role directors are
   now playing in stand-up. (Actually, that is still more than a
   bit self-serving.)

4  *The meta-ending* – well, clearly, I'm doing that in spades.

5  *The QED ending: What have I proved or established?*
   I guess this is the more conventional ending. Here it is:
   The counter-intuitive idea that something as natural

and spontaneous seeming as stand-up can be directed is becoming increasingly accepted. In this book, I have argued that the twin drivers of this have been stand-up courses and Edinburgh shows becoming more theatrically ambitious. (And I work on both sides.) To bring the book full circle (another classic ending device), I'll end by saying: I hope that I have demonstrated that the ultimate solo art form of stand-up can be a truly collaborative endeavour.

# NOTES

## Chapter 1

1  Logan, B. (2015). 'How do you direct a standup gig? Meet the experts behind the comics'. *Guardian*, 24 September. [online] Available at https://www.theguardian.com/stage/2015/sep/24/how-do-you-direct-a-standup-gig-meet-the-experts-behind-the-comics (Accessed 10 January 2017).

2  'Amy Schumer Chats About Her 'Dream Come True' at the Apollo'. (2017). HBO.com. [online] Available at http://www.hbo.com/comedy/amy-schumer-live-from-the-apollo/interview/amy-schumer (Accessed 8 February 2017).

3  Mark, D. (2013). 'Five minutes with ... Milton Jones'. *Wales Online*. [online] Available at http://www.walesonline.co.uk/lifestyle/showbiz/five-minutes-with-milton-jones-1827596 (Accessed 20 March 2017).

4  Wikipedia [online] https://en.wikipedia.org/wiki/Jungian_archetypes (Accessed 3 January 2017).

5  Jones, K. (2014). Laughter is the best medicine: Comedian Francesca Martinez on cerebral palsy. *Express Online*. [online] Available at http://www.express.co.uk/life-style/life/483736/Comedian-Francesca-Martinez-interview-on-cerebral-palsy (Accessed 10 January 2017).

6  Musson, A. (2015). 'Mustard Interview – Stewart Lee'. *Mustard Magazine*. [online] Available at http://www.mustardweb.org/stewartlee/ (Accessed 2 February 2017).

7  'Stewart Lee Interview'. *Totally Dublin*, 9 October. [online] Available at http://totallydublin.ie/more/comedy/interview-stewart-lee/ (Accessed 11 April 2017).

8  'Star Interview: Jack Dee'. (2013). *Northamptonshire Telegraph*, 16 September. [online] Available at http://www.northantstelegraph.co.uk/what-s-on/star-interviews/star-interview-jack-dee-1-5481225 (Accessed 20 January 2017).

# Chapter 2

1 Bill Hicks's *Revelations* can be found here: https://itunes.apple.com/us/movie/bill-hicks-revelations/id1244966522.

# Chapter 3

1 Double, O. (2014). *Getting the Joke: The Inner Workings of Stand-Up Comedy*, 2nd edn. London: Bloomsbury Methuen, p. 432.

# Chapter 4

1 Logan, B. (2017). 'Comedy's Rule Breakers'. *The Guardian*, 8 November. https://www.theguardian.com/stage/2017/nov/08/jordan-brookes-comedy-rule-breakers (Accessed 8 November 2017).

2 Double, *Getting the Joke: The Inner Workings of Stand-Up Comedy*, p. 423.

3 'From Sherlock to Hamlet: Interview with actor Andrew Scott'. *BBC Newsnight* (TV programme), BBC2 3 August 2017 (UK), available at https://www.youtube.com/watch?v=xkcclZoi790.

4 Musson, A. (2015). 'Mustard Interview – Stewart Lee'. *Mustard Magazine*. [online] Available at http://www.mustardweb.org/stewartlee/ (Accessed 2 February 2017).

# Chapter 5

1 Dean, G. (2017). 'Glossary of Stand-up Terms'. [online] Available at https://stand-upcomedy.com/glossary-of-stand-up-comedy-terms/ (Accessed 28 March 2017).

2 All jokes quoted in Chapter 5 (with the exception of W.C. Fields and Oscar Wilde which are public domain) are with permission from UKTV's Dave's Funniest Joke of the Fringe Award. https://corporate.uktv.co.uk/search/?q=Dave%27s+joke+of+the+fringe (accessed various dates 2017).

3 Allen, T. (2002). *Attitude*. London: Gothic Image Publications, p. 42.

4 Gompertz, W. (2012). *What Are You Looking At? 150 Years of Modern Art in the Blink of an Eye.* London: Penguin, p. 3.

5 Murray, L. (2010). *Be a Great Stand-up.* London: Teach Yourself, p. 24.

6 Auton, R. (2013). 'Joke'. [online] Available at http://www.robauton.co.uk/blank-c1paq (Accessed 24 April 2017).

# Chapter 6

1 Richard Lindesay's material is quoted with his kind permission. http://www.richardlindesay.com/

2 Mark Smith's joke quoted with permission from UKTV's Dave's Funniest Joke of the Fringe Award. https://corporate.uktv.co.uk/search/?q=Dave%27s+joke+of+the+fringe (Accessed 19 August 2017).

3 Masai Graham's joke quoted with permission from UKTV's Dave's Funniest Joke of the Fringe Award. https://corporate.uktv.co.uk/search/?q=Dave%27s+joke+of+the+fringe (Accessed 19 August 2017).

# Chapter 7

1 Double, O. (1991). 'An Approach to Traditions of British Stand-Up Comedy'. *Core.* [online] Available at https://core.ac.uk/download/pdf/9554350.pdf (Accessed 1 June 2017).

2 Johnson, S. (2015). 'Every Joke Falls Into One of These Eleven Categories'. *Blink.com.* [online] Available at http://bigthink.com/stephen-johnson/every-joke-falls-in-one-of-these-11-categories-according-to-the-founder-of-the-onion (Accessed 15 May 2017).

3 From Jerry Seinfeld, 'I'm Telling You for the Last Time'; see https://en.wikipedia.org/wiki/I%27m_Telling_You_for_the_Last_Time

# Chapter 8

1 Footage and transcript of the Brian Regan UPS routine can be found here: http://funny-stand-up-comedy-central.blogspot.co.uk/2014/08/brian-regan-ups-trouble-with-girth-and.html.

2 Neil Ackroyd quote via email, 10 April 2017.

# Chapter 9

1 *Trying is Good* is available here: https://www.amazon.co.uk/ Josie-Long-Trying-Good-DVD/dp/B0019ROEPU.
2 Bill Bailey's *Cosmic Jam* is available here: https://itunes.apple.com/gb/ tv-season/bill-bailey-cosmic-jam/id457314831.

# Chapter 10

1 Double, *Getting the Joke: The Inner Workings of Stand-Up Comedy*, p. 393.

# Chapter 11

1 Rabin, N. (2004). 'Chris Rock'. AVClub. [online] Available at http:// www.avclub.com/article/chris-rock-13903 (Accessed 22 March 2017).
2 Musson, A. (2015). 'Mustard Interview: Graham Linehan'. *Mustard Mag*. [online] Available at http://www.mustardweb.org/grahamlinehan/ (Accessed 29 June 2017).

# Chapter 13

1 *The Naked Racist* is available here: https://www.laughingstock.co.uk/ shop/DownloadDetails?rid=LGS_RE_117

# Chapter 14

1 Dineen, D. (2007). 'Both Barrels – an interview with Daniel Kitson'. *The Skinny*. [online] Available at http://www.theskinny.co.uk/ theatre/interviews/both-barrels-an-interview-with-daniel-kitson (Accessed 10 June 2017).

# INDEX